Journey Into Inner Peace

Relaxation & Meditation Healing Rituals

A Time for Nourishing Your Body
Expanding Your Mind
&
Nurturing Your Spirit

Journey Into Inner Peace

Relaxation & Meditation Healing Rituals

Written By
Ivy Shadiah Hylton, MSW, LICSW, D.D.

In this book you will find Ideas to
Detox, Relax and Energize
Create A Sacred Healing Sanctuary in Your Home
Learn How to Prepare for Serenity, Emotional
Balance and Peace of Mind

authorHOUSE®

AuthorHouse™
1663 Liberty Drive
Bloomington, IN 47403
www.authorhouse.com
Phone: 1-800-839-8640

First published by AuthorHouse 10/20/2011

ISBN: 978-1-4520-8560-9 (sc)

Library of Congress Control Number: 2010915073

Printed in the United States of America

*Any people depicted in stock imagery provided by Thinkstock are models,
and such images are being used for illustrative purposes only.
Certain stock imagery © Thinkstock.*

This book is printed on acid-free paper.

Dedication to this journey commits your body, mind and spirit to coordinated healing, rest, relaxation, self analysis, self worth, physical and spiritual wellness.

A total collective expression of

Serenity Living

Contents

Chapter One: In the Beginning There Was Light

Chapter Two: Synergize Your Life

Chapter Three: Accessing the Higher Self

Chapter Four: Emotional Wellness

Chapter Five: Relaxation and Meditation Healing Rituals

Chapter Six: Serenity Living

Meet Rev. Ivy Shadiah Hylton

…..Yesterday, I ascended into the light, and last night I was lifted into flight on the wings of an Angel who's personal revelation, mystical meditation in the form of a sound was a healing for me….As an herbal tincture for the mind, she sings songs of love and hope…She sings her songs of love and hope. She filled our empty ears and kissed our dried up tears with a voice that fills the earth to the sky…and our hearts rhythm is in her song waking up loves bright light…She brings love with the voice of heaven and earth. She sings in the key of faith…unlocking the sounds of loves healing heart beats. She sings of love and hope…Her body glows with spirit inspiration and our bodies vibrate to her love sounds…She is our hope for love…..a mystical meditation…..an angelic revelation, singing in song of spirit love. Brother Bakti (Washington, DC)

Rev. Dr. Ivy Hylton, MSW, LICSW, CHT, D.D. is an internationally known Inspirational Speaker, Soprano Concert Vocalist, Sound Healer, Reiki Master, Reflexologist, Hypnotherapist, and Clinical Consultant in Stress Management, Burnout Prevention, Wellness Education, Strengthening Families, Spirituality,

Integrative Social Work Practice and Emotional Wellness. Her passion is dedicated to mind-body spirit connections, and encouraging compassionate mindfulness all over the world. She is the author of three books, producer and artist of 6 CD's all dedicated to inner peace, emotional balance, rest and relaxation.

As a grief and loss specialist, Rev. Ivy served as a team member of the D.C. Public Schools Grief and Loss Initiative addressing the violence and trauma that youth experience living in the city. She also served as a recovery specialist for United Way during the 9/11 traumatic crises in Washington, D.C. working with families, care givers and schools directly impacted by the trauma. She is on the cutting edge of a new paradigm for psychological, physiological and emotional healing, with a break through concept in the use of Synergistic Sonic Sound and Vibration to teach, inspire and transform. Just as her relative, Marian Anderson, the renowned Contralto vocalist, broke through the barriers of racism to dazzle the world with her powerful and spirit filled voice, Ivy is creating sound and vibration that goes beyond the present use of sound and music, charting a path to new musical practices for wellness, love and healing. "Music is Medicine for the Soul".

Rev. Hylton is a contributing clinical advisor in the Small

Business Innovative Research Grant at the National Cancer Institute- National Institutes of Health, featured as one of the leading integrative therapist in the Nation, on the Complementary Cancer Care: CD-Rom/DVD produced by HealthMark Multimedia, LLC, released 2006. Rev. Ivy is an ordained minister and spiritual healer dedicated to serving as a vessel for releasing the burdens that God never intended us bear. Rev. Ivy's ministry, Healing Temple of light Sanctuary International, is dedicated to the scripture stating; "Come unto me, all of you who are weary and carry heavy burdens, and I will give you rest". (Matt.11:28)

Rev. Ivy Hylton is CEO and founder of Serenity Healing Arts Wellness Education and Holistic Services and proprietor of the Heaven House Retreat for rest and relaxation, in Berkeley Springs West Virginia. In 1989 founded Psychological Support Services Institute in Washington, D.C., a freestanding mental health clinic, and served as Co-Owner and Clinical Director for eight years.

Rev. Ivy has dedicated her life to empowering people towards the realization of inner peace, personal wholeness, total balance and harmony through relaxation, meditation and prayer, specializing in working with women and girls. She is the founder of the Inspirational Women and Girls Empowerment Society, dedicated to providing extraordinary life changing experiences, focused on discovering Soul purpose in life, and commitment to a continuous process of personal healing and service. A pioneer of holistic psychotherapy, Ivy has served as guest lecturer and field instructor in the School of Social Work for the University of Maryland, University of Alabama, Hong Kong University, Lincoln University, Howard University and Delaware State University. She has published articles for local magazines and professional associations and is a member of The National Association of Social Workers and a past President of the METRO Chapter 2002-2004. Rev. Ivy is also a member of the National Association of Black Social Workers and has served as wisdom sage for the National African Centered Social Work Academy; she is also a member of the International Society for Social Work and Spirituality. Ivy has been the opening act for several notable bestselling authors. She opened for Iyanla Vanzant's, book tour, "Tapping the Power Within," African American Women on Tour, as well as for Deepak Chopra, Marion Williamson, Dannion Brinkley, J. California Cooper, Ruby Dee and Sonia Sanchez to name a few.

Rev. Ivy has served as a Sacred Sound Healing Circle facilitator for Inner Visions Worldwide Spiritual Life Maintenance Center, Inc., in Silver Spring, Maryland, the home of Iyanla Vansant, bestselling author, lecturer, radio and television celebrity. Ivy has been a featured workshop facilitator for the Washington National Cathedral Sacred Circles Conference held in 2001 & 2005.

She also served as a resident wellness consultant for Sister Space and Books, located in Washington DC, where she received much of her inspiration and encouragement for publishing. Rev. Ivy has performed European concert tours and has traveled the United States performing and lecturing with the Whole LIFE EXPO and Wisdom Television. She has performed with Bro. Ah's World Music Ensemble and Sounds of Awareness. She is a former member of the Washington Performing Arts Society. Rev. Hylton's music is featured in an award winning independent film entitled Ira & Abby, available now on DVD, and airing on SHOWTIME, The Movie Channel and HBO. Ira and Abby is a film about love, marriage, family, depression, treatment and recovery; starring a cadre of award winning actors and actresses.

Her most recent musical works includes:

- Shadiah and Plunky...Music Medicine for the Soul on Compact Disc;

- Sacred Symphonies...Spirituals, Meditations and music for compassion and healing

- Crystal Dreams…Vibrational Healing Tones of Crystal Bowls on Compact Disc and cassette;

- Sound Vibronics™, Acoustic Brain Wave Entrainment- Sonic Stress Reduction and Chakra Healing Meditation Healing System- (Practice Guide and 2 - Compact Discs set)

- Mind, Body, Spirit…a musical massage on cassette;

- Serenity "Journey into Inner Peace on Compact Disc

- Harmony - Balance - Healing (self-empowerment for Human Services Professionals on Compact Disc and practice guide).

Ivy Hylton has dedicated her life to empowering people towards the realization of inner peace, personal wholeness and total balance in life.

A mother, a wife, a servant and instrument of the Divine Creator.

Introduction

Relaxation and Meditation techniques are natural tools for influencing the process of spiritual, emotional, mental and physical awareness. The practice model for the Journey into Inner Peace is the Synergistic Healing System. The Synergistic Healing System is a process that I discovered during hundreds of hours of meditation, practice and experience over the years of my life and career, seeking to find balance and healing in my own life, as well as assisting others to find the same. This journey can be a life changing transformational process with dedicated practice. As I travel around the world giving retreats and workshops on relaxation and meditation, I am often discovering people that say they do not know how to relax, or that they feel relaxation is not possible for them. Others tell me that they know how to relax and give examples like, reading, watching television or taking part in some type of social or recreational activity. They are all shocked and in disbelief when I tell them that it is possible that those activities may be relaxing, however, it is not experiencing deep levels of true relaxation. Journey into Inner Peace is a collection of healing methods and practices, organized and designed to accomplish a total sense of synergistic wholeness and balance in life. This private collection of Serenity Living healing rituals, now formally known as the Synergistic Healing System, is a brainwave approach to achieving deep levels of relaxation, attaining increased energy levels and improving the overall immune system. Bringing fourth many ideas and contemplative practices that will guide you into inner peace, psychological balance and optimal health. I highly recommend that you use these daily rituals to work on your personal growth and areas of concern in your life. The Synergistic Healing System is designed to serve as an a ' la carte Personal Collection of relaxation techniques, moments of serenity, high energy, mental calmness, exploration of the healing arts and attaining a sense of emotional balance. Inducing relaxation and a relaxed attitude can increase the success of achieving your life's desires and soul purpose on earth. The ability to reach deep levels of relaxation opens the passageway to effective meditation. Relaxation and meditation will strengthen your immune system, increase your energy levels, and improve memory retention while synergistically empowering your entire life! Now we know that the mind/body connection is well established in scientific literature, and has proven some very powerful points of view for attaining wellness. You can use your brain to strengthen your immune system and mobilize the body's natural defense system. Regular use of stress reduction exercises will help alleviate symptoms of anxiety, depression, and nervousness. Physical or emotional symptoms that may be associated with chronic illnesses and their treatment, such as: cancer, hyper tension, HIV/AIDS, cardiovascular (heart) disease, diabetes, migraine headaches, are significantly improved with deep levels of rest, relaxation and meditation.

Practicing meditation can change how you relate to your personal flow of emotional energy and the thoughts that wonder in your mind. Relaxation and Meditation are often used for improving health in what is known as mind-body medicine. Mind – Body medicine focuses on interactions of the brain, the body, the mind and behavior. The first step towards finding inner peace must be through meditation. We cannot have peace without until we find peace within. Relaxation and meditation furnishes the key to unlock the door of inner peace, serenity and emotional balance. The results from learning and the practice of relaxation and meditation can bring a unique understanding of the cries of life, bringing support and divine illumination into being. In making room for relaxation, it is necessary to get rid of tension, which means conflict. Conflict is a major block to relaxation and meditation. Trying to meditate or relax with a mind filled with thoughts of confusion can be very challenging and could be discouraging. Conflict must be overcome by thought (mental capacity) and skill (command of the techniques). These skills and techniques can be developed and mastered to eradicate belittling distractive thoughts, by flooding the mind with thought forms of a positive and divine nature. Action is needed to keep mental awareness cleared of undesirable thoughts. Consistent and rhythmic practice of the Synergistic Healing System will ensure your success. With desire and practice, the mind can focus on a higher consciousness of living. Get out of your own thoughts and into a higher place of thinking and become a self witness of your own personal transformation. See the primary purpose of each and every life experience and draw from the Divine Wisdom of the experience for your own wellness and inner peace.

Research has been done on the brain for many years. The most important point to come from this research is the fact that one side of the brain tends to become cut off from the other, as painful memories and feelings are repressed. For most people, one side will dominate according to what sort of abilities and aptitudes they have, and the cultural influences of their upbringing. Unconscious emotional blocks can freeze huge proportions of our mental energy, and this can cause a person to feel negative, angry, depressed and separated from a sense of inner peace for no apparent reason.

The Synergistic Healing System is designed to support the integration of the left and right brain for improved levels of wellness and oneness of mind, body and spirit.

The ways in which emotional, mental, social, spiritual, and behavioral factors can directly affect health is a real significant truth. Negative stress is a killer of life and relaxation and meditation is a giver of life. It is time to take the time to rest for a while and allow the peaceful vibrations of synergistic healing to overwhelm your soul and penetrate your mind for Inner Peace and Serenity.

Journey into Inner Peace will guide you into deep levels of relaxation, creating an environment in your home, work and inner sanctuary that will serve to support the healing of your heart, mind and spirit. Get into the habit of mentally remembering the feelings that you induce during deep relaxation and formalize a mental picture of yourself relaxed and at inner peace at all times, no matter what is going on in your life. These lessons help to recall the relaxed sensations experienced during deep relaxation and meditation by creating a sacred space for personal healing. Relaxation will reduce fatigue and better enable you to handle tension from daily life circumstances. Meditation is a practice of quieting the mind to allow mental clarity and stress reduction. Meditation allows you to become serene and eternally endowed with inner peace.

Continued meditation, will develop a natural buffer to your daily stressors. Meditation is achieving a state of No Mind; letting go of the mind and retraining the mind to be emotionally free from distracting thoughts. Relaxing the body certainly helps in allowing one to enter swiftly into a state of meditativeness. However, relaxation cannot be termed as meditation. The more relaxed the mind is, the deeper you can enter into meditation. The more deeply you can enter into meditation, all the more relaxed the mind and body becomes. It is like an ongoing cycle. One facilitates the other. Relaxing and maintaining a positive perspective will alleviate tension and anxiety that interferes with the efficient functioning of your body temple.

In time, your relaxed attitude will become a natural part of your lifestyle, and you will no longer need to consciously practice it. Relaxation not only is pleasurable but also allows our bodies to re-establish it's natural rhythms, emotional behavioral patterns , internal order and increased immune system functioning. Complete relaxation comes from the elimination of stress and tension within our minds and bodies, thereby creating a total sense of serenity and inner peace within the spirit. Relaxation techniques will not eliminate *all* causes of stress and tension; however, it will eliminate with faithful practice, the primary symptoms of stress and tension (i.e., shallowness of breath, muscular tension, eye strain, headaches, worries etc.). Slowly, as relaxation and meditation becomes natural, you may actually experience the awareness of relaxation penetration deep within your body. Everyone is affected by various degrees of stress. Those who work and live in toxic and polluted environments are more likely to profoundly experience the symptoms of negative stress. While stress may cause useless fatigue initially, it is dangerous to your overall optimal health over time. The physical body is designed to handle stressful situations, however; continued, excessive chronic stress can lead to illness, unhappiness, accidents, sickness, disease and/ or distress. While a certain amount of stress can never be avoided, you must maintain a strong immune system to resist its negative effects. Negative distressful Stress is a release of poisonous toxins into the body, resulting into a combination of vaporous gases into the endocrine glandular system. This chemical reaction is often time undetectable, and most likely to result into discomfort and pain or other symptoms of stress related illnesses, resulting into weakening of the human Aura.

The Journey into Inner Peace will guide you onto a path of strengthening your Aura and creating an ethereal counter response to the vaporous poisons of stress. The Aura is an invisible breath, emanation, or radiation of light force energy surrounding the human bio energy field. Research done by Dr. Valerie Hunt has shown how the human body is first impacted at the spiritual level (aura) before the physical body responds. She states that disturbed bioelectric fields develop cancer faster; lower immune responses, create more migraines, allergies, neuromuscular pains, eye strain and emotional "ups and downs". The bio energy field is a distinctive but intangible quality of the human experience that seems to surround a person or thing around the atmosphere.

Strengthening the Aura by treating the bio energy field, counters the effects of negative stress, trauma and chaotic states of world-wide trauma. You must attain the ability to acquire a higher consciousness designed to change your perspective of life in order to actualize inner peace. In short, you must become enlightened. Failure to manage stress can result in the development of major diseases or, in some cases, even death.

Albert Einstein said, "That it is not possible to solve a problem within the same consciousness that produced it". Therefore, it is necessary to obtain a new level of consciousness to attain success in life and resolve problems that seem to repeat themselves over and over again.

To create a significant paradigm shift in ones behavior, you must first experience a major shift in self-consciousness, self-knowledge, self-control, and creating a disciplined imagination. The objective of the Serenity living philosophy of life is to create conditions in which one can experience deep, deep levels of relaxation, which prepares the mind (brain) for positive suggestion, emotional intelligence and increased memory retention. The assumption is that life's pressures and associated stressor's are unavoidable. We assume that based upon our physiology (i.e. the endocrine system) our bodies are designed to handle stress when properly educated on how to access control. Therefore, the goal should not be to avoid stress, since challenges can stimulate evolution, growth and understanding. The goal is to attain a higher level of consciousness, self-awareness, skill and personal responsibility. We cannot blame stress for poor health and mental distress. Rather, we become more susceptible to stress because of poor health. In short, we experience stress-related symptoms because we have not taken the steps to maintain stress coping mechanisms within our physiology, rational mind and inner spirit. During periods of deep relaxation, the mind, which is part of the invisible body, can impress ideas, and thoughts upon the brain. The Synergistic Healing System's philosophy of practice involves gaining an in-depth understanding of how the brain functions and how to induce brain wave levels that instantly control the emotions and allow the body to go into relax instantaneously.

As we seek to soar further into the new age of higher

consciousness...we must realize that this is the era of spirituality, and the realization of the development for optimal mind/ body wellness, and spiritual enlightenment. This state of awareness can be attained through the power of inner peace, and freedom from the emotional perils of negative life conditions. The ability to separate the self from the outward stresses of life circumstances is the primary intention of your Journey into Inner Peace. The famous saying that "The kingdom of Heaven is within you", is the most accurate description of where inner peace resides. It is also, however, the most elusive experience we will realize in our personal lifetime.

When you look around in your community and even deep within your own family, you will see that health issues, substance abuse, mental illness, heart disease, high blood pressure, diabetes, and obesity, to name a few, have all become very prevalent. Many *dis-eases* are showing up and challenging the very essence of our personal and family lifestyles as well as our day to day relationships.

Dis-Stress has played, and continues to play, a major role in tearing down the human body, mind and spirit. The dis-ease of the spirit is the primary cause of the physical breakdown of the body, and the inability to attain inner peace. This has been proven by several research projects around the world as well as the National Institutes of

Health (NIH) USA. This relaxation and meditation healing system has been designed to allow time for movement to increase your energy flow and to practice a synergistic system of daily rituals that will enhance your quality of living. You will enhance your thinking and spiritual consciousness abilities to love yourself even more. I am convinced that self-love is the key to total happiness in life. I am also convinced that many of us do not understand the path to self love. We believe that we do love ourselves…however, how often are we in total bliss and realizing our hearts deepest desires? The path to self-love is embedded deeply within the subconscious awareness of Soul purpose and the still small voice within. Developing the ability to provide deep introspection will reveal the stillness that allows us to hear the voice of God within. Being in touch with this voice allows us to live a less stressful life, and we can then begin to realize total optimal wellness and healing. The path which leads to the ability to become aware of this voice requires us to reach our deepest levels of relaxation and meditation. When we are able to release the ego and allow the God force presence to ascended, the experience of serenity and bliss can be actually realized. Even if it is only for a few moments, it is worth the opportunity to feel free of everyday burdens, while increasing higher inner levels of wellness, love and purpose in life.

Take time to read this self-help book to ensure proper use of the rituals within the Journey to Inner Peace. Together we will discover, practice and share Inner Peace, Emotional Balance and the Power of the Mind.

Stay in the light of Love,

Ivy

Acknowledgements and Special Thanks
"I am so grateful"

One day, about 19 years ago, I was in the studio singing the *Inner Peace Movement Song* with a singing group that I started called SPELLBOND. When I became aware that I was no longer in control of my voice, the sounds and vibrations that were emanating from within me had become one with the instruments and my spirit had transformed itself into actual sound and movement. I felt totally free from the confines of my physical body; I felt oneness of mind and spirit that I had never known before. In that brief instant, my ego was released and it felt as though I had become embraced with pure light, love and a state of inner peace. I was vibrating within Gods frequency of communication and understanding, and I knew it, I absolutely knew at that very moment that the presence of GOD is within us. In that moment I could hear the voice of God speaking to me and giving me orders to pay attention to the power of sound and vibration for healing the world.

During this time in my life, I was in the infant stages of connecting the use of the ancient power of sound and how it can transform, elevate and eliminate stress and pain from the human body. Totally unaware that divine knowing in my mind is a scientific truth. In 1994 the final musical version of Synergy Movement and Sound Meditation was completed and I knew the time had come to share this powerful Secret with the world. However, it was not until my spiritual sista, Rabia Rayford, poetess extraordinaire, (may she rest in peace) came into my life and encouraged me to get the "*little books of wisdom*" out of my mind and into book form for worldwide readership. Just before she made her transition in 2007, she told me that "Journey into Inner Peace should flow with words that speak of love, inspiration, and beautiful thoughts". I would like to give thanks to Akili Ron Anderson, an African Art Icon, who inspired me to explore my visual art talents and create my own art images for the book. My sister girl friend Yvette Benjamin "FREE", songstress, guitarist and master Graphic Artist took my vision for the cover and created the perfect image for this journey.......FREE I am so grateful to you my sister love. Sister Faye Williams, founder and proprietor of Sister Space and Books was the first inspiration in my life to become an author and share my gifts with the world. I must also acknowledge my son Richard, who gave me my first opportunities to experience the power of vibrational healing. Finally, I would like to recognize my husband, Saleem Hylton, for sharing and enduring the many moments, hours and unpredictability of my creative thoughts and energies, and for accepting me for who and all that I am.

The original concept of the pictures came to me in 1981, while I was living in Cleveland, Ohio. A young artist drew the initial concept for me and I kept it with me now for just over thirty years. When the details of the images for the book began to visually appear to me, I felt as though my hands were being guided by spiritual forces that were determined to bring forth artistic talents heretofore not experienced by me. I also knew that the spirit had decided that it was time for my creative energies to be redefined.

I would like to express my deepest gratitude and gratefulness for the patience, endurance, trust and inspiration received from my original supporters for the Journey into Inner Peace; Inspirational Woman Allie Bird and Sister Joanna Banks. You were the first to believe in my vision and I will never forget. Without Allie and Joanna's support and determination to believe in me, this work would not have been possible. I would like to say to my sister friend, Iyanla Vanzant, thank you for your support and love over the years and offering your words of inspiration and encouragement on this back cover of this book. To my St. Croix, Virgin Island supporters who never gave up on me, I offer this shout out for your love, heartfelt support, prayers and determination to believe in me and my Ministry of Healing.

I would like to first thank Rev. Richard Austin and his lovely wife Nolly from the Beulah African Methodist Epistical Zion Church of the St Croix, Virgin Islands support crew, for bringing the St. Croix family together to help cheer me on and celebrate the coming of this project with faith in God and endurance. I would like to express my deepest and sincerest heartfelt love and appreciation for Dr. ChenziRa Kahina, who came all the way from St Croix Virgin Islands to Heaven House Retreat, West Virginia to push me over the top for completion of Journey in Inner Peace. May you enjoy your lovely healing herbal salt bath after staying up all night with me to get the final work done.

The following individuals are members of the St, Croix Support Crew that offered me love, understanding, trust and patience. You are very special to me; Nest Dr. Chenzira, Aloy Nielsen, Mary Grant, Rita Robertson, Claudette Young-Hinds, Renee' Blakey, Rigmerle Finch, Winnie Loving(my sister Oyoko), Stephanie Malanga, Francine Cruickshank, Eurkres Rallings, Florence C. Petersen, Tonia Tyrell, Noelia B. Austin, Marin Roebuck.

Welcome to the first in a series of "The Little Books of Wisdom". I invite you to take a *wisdom journey* with me and let the spirit move you to a higher physical, emotional and spiritual plane.

Transforming Life into Balance

In June of 1989, the healing work of transformation became a concentrated focus of my work as a holistic psychotherapist, when I realized that symptoms of depression are manifestations of the transformational process of the human soul, and not just merely a pathological diagnosis for "emotional and psychological dysfunction". It became very clear to me that a systematic approach to the transformational process was needed to assist my clients through some very painful life experiences. I was asked to write a column for a local magazine, (The CeCe Guide, Washington DC). The Column was entitled *Transforming Life into Balance*. This led me into a deeper analysis and practice of transformational work as a Psychotherapist, Reiki Master, Spiritual and Sound Healer. I conducted an eight-week course on Transformation at Sister Space and Books, located in Washington DC, and that is when I discovered the connection to the soul and personal transformation. For eight weeks some twenty sisters and I, came together every Saturday morning to travel the spiritual, transformational journey together. Each week we discovered that most of our life experiences were similar, but having had different circumstances.

We prayed together, cried together, lay hands on one another, conducted water and sound rituals, experienced healing and discovered our *true selves*, as we each became transformed in the transformational process. One of the most profound discoveries made during this time was the realization that when we have trauma in our lives, it stores in the cells, organs and emotional body. Through the transformation rituals, healing was found. In order to heal, a restoration of the cells is required to realize optimal wellness. The Transformational Healing Rituals offered to our minds, bodies and souls a call for *wholeness*. It is crucial to understand that the journey towards inner healing must be recognized as not a cure, but however, a sacred communication process of the Soul. It was during my time spent with the women at Sister Space and books, located in Washington DC, that I realized my life lessons had to be told. The inspiration of the many female African American authors that I had the pleasure of meeting, have served as my source of energy and determination to express myself in the form of written words to inspire others.

State the following words out loud in a meaningful and bold way: "I love and approve of myself exactly as I am. I am attractive, brilliant, considerate, dependable, energetic, and focused. I am on the journey towards healing and reconditioning my mind for *transformation* and inner peace. The attainment of prosperity, love, peace, joy and self-approval are my missions. I am *releasing* the old and making room for the new. My heart is now open for love and healing. By releasing and forgiving negative experiences from the past, my eyes can only see the good in others and myself. My mouth will only speak positive vibrations."

These are transformational thought patterns; affirmations for reconditioning the mind to eliminate negative mental conditions like criticism, anger, fear, jealousy, resentment and guilt. The mind, body and spirit are interconnected and programmed for personal transformation into soul balance. The soul is a spiritual matrix pattern woven deeply into the DNA, nerve fibers, cellular tissue, glands and genes of each organ in the body. The *soul matrix* is creating a sacred communication process with the creator defining *soul purpose* in life, and receiving guidance on how to actualize that purpose. Transformation is a metamorphosis or the act of being transformed. The caterpillar transforms into a butterfly, negative thoughts are transformed into positive thoughts, and the human being is transformed into Soul Purpose and Inner Peace.

Transformation indicates a change in conditions, appearance and character. So what is the process of spiritual transformation? The primary components to Spiritual Transformation are:

- **CONCENTRATION** – The ability to pay close attention. The strength of a soul union.

- **CONTEMPLATION** – The act of looking at or thinking about something positive for long periods of time. From contemplation, one can become wise with the creation of deep thought forms.

- **MEDITATION** – Quiet no-thoughts in action, inner reflection, contemplation on sacred or solemn subjects, especially as a devotional exercise. The ability to be still and just allow yourself to be present in the moment.

- **PRAYER** – A form of words to be used in praying. One of the principle forms of worship. Be prayerful and develop a habit for prayer and quiet listening for the still small voice within. Talking to GOD.

- **FOCUS** – The clear and well-defined state of an image. Maintain an attitude of intense focus on a central idea related to your soul purpose in life. Intense focus brings a thought to a point of clarity and creates the pathway for pristine images to appear. Be a "focuser" in the process of transformation.

BALANCE – The condition of being equal in weight, amount, force and effects. Bringing something into, or keep it in a steady condition or position. Balance is a sign of quiet temperament, which is the mark of a balanced and wise person. Balance denotes a sort of equilibrium point between two positions, illustrated in the image of the scales. We are in balance when we get two or more things to balance, like trying to balance your body while standing on one leg. When we are in balance, we have found a position that keeps us steadily moving forward without stopping, falling or doubting one 's self. Due to the fact that staying balanced is a "balancing act", the threat of losing balance is always present. There is always the possibility that something will unbalance us and cause us to fall. We are always at risk when we are balancing things to face the tumbling down that comes after the inability to maintain equilibrium. When things get out of rhythm or out of balance, we can fall. But we can get back up and regain our balance. Balance is always a possibility.

HARMONY - Finding harmony means finding ways to live harmoniously. Facing everyday conflicts of diverse people living together in a world defined by scarcity, economic crises and fear, harmony is a pathway towards creatively finding solutions to re-establishing connectedness. Harmonious living is the very basic necessity to work together, to collaborate and to be aligned with the larger objectives of the whole scheme of humanity. No living system is productive without a harmony among its being and intention. No nation can be strong and solvent without a harmony among its people. We all know that harmonious living is essential for growth, for pleasure and for happiness. However, what we haven't found are better, sustainable and equitable ways to live harmoniously. That is what this Journey into Inner Peace proposes to explore, discover and share.

The transformational process of harmony, balance and inner peace requires a total body relaxation response. Attention must be given to creating intentional relaxation daily. The use of Synergy Music Medicine, created by yours truly, is capable of creating the perfect alpha/Theta brain waves necessary for total body *mind *spirit relaxation.

THE FIRST TRANSFORMATIONAL HEALING RITUAL ON THIS JOURNEY

Play quiet synergistic spiritually inspired instrumental background music. As the music is playing softly, begin to hum to it quietly for a few moments. Focus your attention on your heart until you feel the vibration centered in your heart. Place your hands over your heart and imagine that the vibrations you feel in your heart are sending soothing vibrations to every cell, muscle and organ of your body, bringing the body into a state of equilibrium. Breathe deeply for two minutes very slowly through the nose, and then exhale through the nose. Listen deeply for guidance from your heart. During this ritual I suggest that you practice Sensorium Sound Meditation, by adding the essential oil rose to your experience. Place one drop of the rose oil in the palm of your hands and briskly rub your hands together. Place one finger tip drop of the roe oil directly onto your heart, and rub the oil onto the heart in the shape of a spiral circle. Take in the aroma as you breathe and practice the Journey into Inner Peace initial transformational ritual. As you receive mental guidance from your heart, begin to visualize the message as you continue to allow your body to go deeper and deeper into relax. At this time you will begin the Spiritual Transformation process in order. Begin with Concentration and end with Harmony. When you feel that the meditation is complete, slowly bring yourself out of the experience and gently open your eyes. This is the recommended ritual to do whenever you feel that balance, harmony, focus and clarity is needed in your life, as you enjoy your Journey into Inner Peace.

For more clarity regarding the personal transformational process it is important to practice Sensorium Sound Meditation daily. Sensorium Sound Meditation is a process of meditation with toning, aromatherapy, visualization, hydration therapy (water) and oxygenation therapy (the breath), all of which you learn about during your Journey.

I invite you to join me on this Journey into Inner Peace and Emotional Balance. Inside you will find detailed instructions on just how to accomplish these rituals. You can add your own ideas and create new Serenity living ideas as you go along.

Remember to maintain a constructive mental attitude and avoid destructive self-talk while living with direct intentional purpose, on your Journey into Inner Peace.

May God bless you with inner peace and emotional balance.

Transformation and Emotional Balance is yours forever......... Ase'

Chapter One

In the Beginning There Was Light

Vital Energy Centers of the Body

To find Inner Peace and Serenity, you must have the ability to listen to your soul, follow your heart mind and obtain a comprehensive understanding of the vital energy centers of the human body. Energy centers are best known as the *Chakras* (an Indian Sanskrit word meaning wheel or disc) or the original ancient African wisdoms of the "Seven Powers" (psycho-spiritual energy centers of the body temple). A vortex of life force energy gathered together deeply embedded within the body at seven specific points (the endocrine gland system). According to the definition in the Wikipedia, the **endocrine system** is an integrated system of small organs that involve the release of extracellular signaling molecules known as hormones. The endocrine system is instrumental in regulating metabolism, tissue, and also plays a part in determining mood.

The presence of subtle energy is undetectable by the

naked eye or even x-ray. We know that it is there by the feelings we get inside, like butterflies, shortness of breath, frog in the throat, etc. Working with the chakra system of healing is a passageway to attaining enlightenment, vitality, balance, optimal health and inner peace.

There is a complete scientific explanation of the chakra system that is available in numerous books and on the internet. In this book, however, it is my intention to introduce you into the ancient wisdom of the healing energy centers of the body. I encourage you to also seek more in-depth insight for your own healing and spiritual growth. The origin of Psycho-Spiritual Energy Centers is inscribed in the great hieroglyphics found in the pyramids in Egypt. The inscriptions speak very profoundly about the constitution of the human spirit or the vital life force energy found embedded into the spinal cord, also known as the "Kundalini Energy". The Journey into Inner Peace must begin with a basic understanding of the source of pure serenity and inner peace, the inner self, (the various levels of mental consciousness), the true place of the living God within. To attain this higher sense of awareness, it is essential that one understands that the mind must be in state of peace and harmony. The healing system of the *chakras* is what I like to call the "Language of the Soul". When interpreted, you gain insight into the areas of your life necessary to make changes for inner peace and emotional balance. The *chakras* are the centers of the Endocrine System of the human body. The glands of the endocrine system and hormonal releases influence almost every cell, organ, and function of our bodies. The endocrine system is instrumental in regulating mood, growth, development, tissue function, and metabolism; as well as sexual function and reproductive processes. In general, the endocrine system is in charge of body processes that happen slowly, such as cell growth.

Faster processes like breathing and body movement are controlled by the nervous system. However, even though the nervous system and endocrine system are separate systems, they often work together to help the body function properly. An imbalance in the endocrine system can result into serious harm to the body. Obtaining a comprehensive understanding of the Chakras or learning a fundamental interpretation of what I call the "Soul Language" can lead to improved health and significant spiritual enlightenment.

The **first chakra** is located at the base of the spine. It is associated with survival, sexuality and being grounded to the earth. Its healing element is earth and the vibrational healing tone is in the key of C. The associated color is red. The **second chakra** is located in the lower navel or abdomen. It is associated with emotions and relationships.

The healing element is water and the vibrational healing tone is in the key of D. The color is orange. The **third chakra is** located in the solar plexus. It is associated with personal power, mental energy, transformation, beliefs and decisions. Its healing element is fire. The vibrational healing tone is in the key of E. The color is yellow. The **fourth chakra** is located at the center of the chest cavity. The heart chakra is associated with love, touch, divine conscious love, understanding and wisdom. The capacity to love and receive love is a primary function of the heart chakra. The heart chakra is a source of building the capacity for compassion, forgiveness, acceptance, inner peace and harmony. Its healing element is air. The vibrational healing tone is in the key of F. The color is green. The secondary color is pink. The **fifth chakra** is located at the center of the throat. The throat chakra is associated with creativity, communication, self expression and the will of God. Its healing element is sound and the vibrational healing tone is in the Key of G. The color is blue. The **sixth chakra** is located at the center of the forehead. The third eye or brow chakra is associated with intuitiveness, imagination, spiritual insight, inner vision and clairvoyance. Its healing element is light. The vibrational healing tone is in the key of A. The color vibration is indigo. The third eye is a primary function in meditation. The brow chakra is the place where your attention is focused and the ability to quiet thoughts and evoke a command of stillness in the body and mind.

The seventh chakra is located at the top of the head. The crown chakra is associated with wisdom, knowledge and understanding- a direct connection with the Divine Mind. The healing element is thought. The vibrational healing tone is in the key of B. The color is violet. The violet ray is a powerful source of healing energy. Visualization of the violet ray connects you with the divine presence of God. It allows for a direct connection into the inner voice of God and the universal cosmos.

The chakras are the healing *pathways* to total consciousness and enlightenment. They provide an opportunity to examine ourselves for finding inner peace and mental clarity. When the body is in tune, we operate with more efficiency, clarity and power.

Additional Energy Centers Connected with the Main Seven Powers of the Human Spirit

The crown chakra is located exactly in the center of the crown of head. The third eye (located between the two eyebrows). The eyes, located in line with the pupil of the eye, just behind the eyeball). The center of the temples located directly above the ear. Base of skull (at the back of the head at the point the spine and skull meet). Roof of the mouth (located where the tongue meets at the roof of the mouth).

The jaw, located at the hinges of the joint in front of the lower edge of the jaw.

The throat Chakra, located just above the breast bone at the base of the neck. The shoulder located at the end of the collarbone.

The center of the shoulder blade, located inside of the blade facing the chest. The arms, elbows, wrist joints and finger joints are all energy centers of the human body.

The solar plexus chakra is a primary energy center. The secondary center is located just below the breast bone. The soft spot down the middle of the breastbone is also an energy center connected to the solar plexus chakra.

The spine, located from the base of the skull to the tailbone requires special attention and consistent manipulation.

The entire pelvic girdle, anus and rectum are all critical energy centers. This entire area is good for relieving constipation and consistent stimulation can help to prevent colon cancer.

The knee joint, located in the center of the knee, beneath the tendons in a circular motion is a major concern for many with knee pain and stiffness.

The ankle, located directly on the ankle bone and the muscle connecting the foot to the ankle.

Tarsal and metatarsals (all the places between the small bones of the foot the toes, heal, the arch and ball of foot).

The energy centers of the body are the focal points for all Synergy Movements. Spend time mentally focusing on these centers so that the releasing of tension can flow with ease.

Chakra Healing System Associated Glands

The major glands that make up the human endocrine system are the hypothalamus, pituitary, thyroid, parathyroids, adrenals, pineal body, and the reproductive glands, which include the ovaries and testes. The pancreas is also part of this hormone-secreting system, even though it is also associated with the digestive system because it also produces and secretes digestive enzymes. Although the endocrine glands are the body's main hormone producers, some non-endocrine organs — such as the brain, heart, lungs, kidneys, liver, thymus, skin, and placenta — also produce and release hormones. In the process of learning and practicing the Synergistic Healing System, it is critical that you gain a comprehensive understanding of the function of each gland, which represents the subtle energies of the Chakras.

The study of the chakra system and the function of the Endocrine System is the Soul Language of the human body, mind and spirit (the "Tri-Consciousness of human existence). When you have mastered the concept of the chakras and their functions, you will have learned the ultimate language of the Soul.

#1-REPRODUCTIVE ORGANS...... Control pelvic area, sex organs, potency, fluid functions, kidneys and bladder. (The Root Chakra)

#2-ADRENALS....Controls all solid parts, spinal column, bones, teeth, nails, anus, rectum, colon, prostate gland, blood and building of cells. (Sacral/Spleen Chakra)

#3-PANCREAS.......Controls liver, digestive system, stomach, spleen, gall bladder, autonomic nervous system, lower back, muscles. (The Solar Plexus)

#4-THYMUS.........Controls heart, blood circulation, immune system, lower lungs, ribcage, skin, upper back, hands. (The Heart Chakra)

#5-THYROID.........Controls jaw, neck, throat, voice, airways, upper lungs, nape of neck, arms. (The Throat Chakra)

#6-PTIUITARY.......Controls endocrine system left brain, left eye, nose, ears, sinuses and parts of the nervous system. (The Third Eye)

#7-PINEAL...........Controls cerebrum, right brain and central nervous system, right eye. (The Crown Chakra)

The Equation for Successful Meditation

Find a peaceful quite place + Close your eyes....Breathe deeply + Select a word or sacred phrase that feels good to you + Repeat your sacred phrase with every exhalation of the breath = MEDITATION

You Can Learn How to Meditate in A Matter of Just A Few Moments of Concentration and Very Simple Techniques.

Meditation

The practice of meditation has occurred worldwide since ancient times in a variety of contexts. It may serve purely as a means for creating quietistic aims, as in the case of many spiritual mystics; it may be viewed as spiritually or physically restorative and enriching to daily life, as in the case of numerous religious orders and the majority of basic meditation practitioners; or it may serve as special, potent preparation for a particular, usually physically or otherwise strenuous activity, as in the case of the warrior before battle or the musician before performance. In recent medical and psychological studies, meditation techniques have proven effective in skilled practitioners in controlling pulse and respiratory rates. Meditation can induce symptomatic control of migraine headaches, hypertension and stress related illness. Meditation is the mental energy of consciousness and change, building cognitive knowing from the power of words, thought and intention. Meditation encourages whole body knowing, the release of mental congestion and creates sacred space for personal healing. Meditation in its simplest form is the ability to transcend for a few moments and experience deep rest of mind, body and spirit. It is a method of clearing thoughts from the mind and absorbing a natural energy that can last indefinitely. It is a spiritual and physical inner experience.

Meditation should be practiced at least twice a day for 10-20 minutes. Always sit in an upright position, spine erect with arms resting on your thighs, palms facing upward. Begin with taking deep cleansing breaths through the nostrils and slowly exhale through the nostrils. Slowly close the eyes as you exhale to the count of ten. Your body should remain absolutely still and relaxed as you take repeated deep breaths. Hold it for a moment and exhale slowly.....and now allow your breath to become normal without a conscious effort. Just let it happen as you breathe in...and out...very slowly. As you take deep cleansing breaths, allow each breath to release completely into your abdomen naturally, filling your diaphragm completely with air. Gradually begin to focus your awareness on the center of your chest. Allow your thoughts to come and go mindfully, as if you are watching a movie screen... not concentrating on any one thought. Just let the thoughts flow....Ultimately the mind becomes still and clear. Do these for about 5 minutes without watching your watch....just let it happen....changing your focus to the center of your forehead. Focus all of your attention and energy on the center of the forehead with rhythmic deep breaths. Hold the deep breaths for about 3 seconds and then release the breath. Repeat these instructions up to ten times or until you feel a sense of euphoric lightness in your body and mind. The completion of the meditation exercise is focused on relaxing the muscles of the body.

Begin by relaxing the right arm and then left arm…make a tight fist and then tense the entire arm (left & Right) and then release. Relax the right and left upper arm…. by tensing and then releasing. Continue this process with every other muscle from the forehead, face, neck, shoulders and back….to the stomach, thighs, knees, calves, feet and toes.

Just let go of the hold in your muscles and remember to relax the muscles. When you have completed the meditation exercise, bring yourself back slowly by deep breathing and slowly moving your feet, toes, arms, fingers, neck and shoulders. At the end of this exercise, begin to slowly open your eyes, and give thanks.

Relaxation & Meditation
Creates Mental Clarity

CREATING THE PROPER ATMOSPHERE FOR PRACTICING MEDITATION

- ✓ Select a place in your home where you will not be disturbed. A place of quiet solitude.

- ✓ Disconnect the phones and tell everyone in the home that you are in meditation.

- ✓ Establish meditation rules of practice in your home.

- ✓ Create an alter space for meditation and prayer. It is suggested that you have fresh flowers, a seven day white candle in a glass holder and aromatherapy essential oils.

- ✓ Sacred smoke, an ancient art of smudging the room is a popular practice with the use of frankincense and myrrh and other exquisite resins from the earth. Smudging is the burning of herbs or incense as a sacred practice as a purifying agent of the air and a powerful healing tool for meditation. It helps to connect to the higher power by creating an effect on the cranial nerves connected to the neuro-sensory cells of the nasal mucous membrane and then passes on to the anterior part of the cerebrum (brain).

- ✔ Spiritually inspired music playing in the background or simply use the silence. I highly recommend that you use Ivy's meditation healing music for your meditation ritual. www.cdbaby.com/all/ivyhylton

- ✔ Practice meditation in a sitting position. Both feet flat on the floor, hands resting on your lap with palms facing upward. Body must be erect but comfortable.

- ✔ Use a high back chair or sit in the lotus position on the floor.

- ✔ During meditation, when your mind wonders off affirmations, your mantra or thoughts of God, focus your attention on the center of your forehead, the third eye, or your mind's eye of the soul. This will help to maintain your meditation experience.

- ✔ Meditate in the same place each day. Use the same chair and wear comfortable clothing.

- ✔ Meditate at the same time each day. Daily meditation at 6am and then 6 pm for example.

- Avoid meditation after a meal or if you are hungry.

- Avoid meditation in a room filled with the aroma of cooking food or other distractions.

- Practice deep breathing before meditation. It aids in circulation of blood and fosters spiritual cleaning of the mind, body and spirit.

- Drink plenty of water before and after meditation, at least one 8 oz glass.

CHAPTER TWO

Synergize Your Life

Synergy Movement Sound Meditation Ritual

MIND * BODY * SPIRIT

Synergy **M**ovement **S**ound **M**editation is simultaneous body movement with rhythmic sound, contemplation, concentration, meditation and the breath. Daily practice with the MIND * BODY * SPIRIT ritual can lead to increased energy levels, less anxiety and more relaxed and creative living. Deep breathing synergistically with the body and mind to music renews the spirit and uplifts the soul. It also stimulates energy centers in the body to release stress and blockages. Energy centers are major relay stations of the body, where life currents are moving and flowing through the system for regulation. Many of these gateways are located at the joints, or the actual space located between the bones of a joint as mentioned earlier in the chapter on Energy Centers. These energy centers must be felt with the mind. These energy centers are what the etheric body or subtle energy body is made up of. Once you become familiar with your energy centers mentally, you are well on your way to releasing built up tension, stress and dis-ease that has accumulated in the body over the years.

Once you try this healing method, you will immediately feel a body shift in a positive direction of inspiration and encouragement.

Synergy **M**ovement **S**ound **M**editation **R**itual encourages rhythmic movements for increased energy, stress release and inner peace. Synergy music is a revolutionary new concept in the laws of physics, which indicate that our bodies resonate to sound. Every organ in the body resonates to a specific musical note. The primary areas in the body and glands affected are the pineal gland, hair, top of head, central nervous system, pituitary, hypothalamus, eyes, autonomic nervous system, thyroid, parathyroid, neck, ears, respiratory system, throat, thymus, lungs, heart, lymph immune system, pancreas, stomach, liver, small intestine, blood, digestive system, spleen, ovaries, adrenals, kidney, testes, tailbone, legs and feet. These energy centers are the body - mind healing tools available to you when properly functioning and effectively stimulated synergistically.

Preparing for the Synergy Movement Experience

Allow the body and mind to simultaneously move to the rhythmic sounds of the synergy music with a flow of correct breathing. The mind, a creative instrument and spiritual channel through which the body can be healed, should first be directed to be still and focused on the music. When the mind and body energy centers become one with the music, gently close your eyes and melt into each note until you find your body flowing with the symphonic melodies. With each movement, find yourself becoming less and less conscious of your body; just allow it to happen naturally. Flow synergistically with the music while breathing deeply, renewing your spirit and uplifting your soul.

Without breath there is no life

Movement Meditation and the Breath

We must breathe for vitality, for power, for existence, for inner peace for love. Oxygen, the elixir of life is one of the best blood purifiers on earth and one of the most effective nerve tonics freely provided by nature. The breath will bring to you new strength and vitality. It will produce a happy and cheerful attitude of the mind. It will change your negative point of view to a more positive outlook. Creating the habit of deep breathing will help you sleep better, think more clearly, improve blood circulation and a better feeling you all over. The breath touches the very center of your being. The breath is food for the spirit. Synergize your breath with the following instructions for correct breathing.

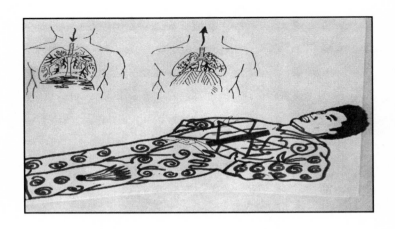

The Deep Breathing Response Exercise

The purpose of deep breathing (diaphragmatic breathing) is simply to calm emotions, increase blood circulation and set the mood for a relaxed state and/or restful sleep. It is suggested to do this exercise in one or two ways. You can do it lying down flat or sitting in a comfortable chair. Be sure that your clothing is loose and free of any tightness. If you decide to sit, be sure that your hands are comfortably to your side or resting on your thighs and your back (spine) or straight out, not strained. If you decide to choose lying on your back, be sure to bend your knees placing your feet as close to the buttocks as possible. This will relive tension in the lower back area if necessary.

Begin breathing through the nostrils...inhale deeply to the count of ten and expand your abdomen like a balloon to the count of ten. Remember to relax your shoulders and chest while breathing. Slowly exhale through the nostrils while drawing in the abdomen as flat as you can, moving the diaphragm only to the count of ten. With practice you will be able to control your breathing while maintaining a steady breath pattern.

When you properly use the lungs, your capacity for using more air increases, vitality increases, mental congestion is relieved and more oxygen is released to the brain for improved mental clarity. A relaxed lifestyle is dependent upon the regular and adequate supply of oxygen than any other life element. A very important change takes place in the blood as it passes through the lungs. The blood is returned in the veins from all parts of the body directly into the right side of the heart. Forming the habit of deep breathing will make you sleep better, think more clearly, have better blood circulation and make you feel better all over. Deep breathing is more beneficial when you can breathe fresh air. Regular trips to the mountains and beach offers a great source of fresh air for deep breathing. Oxygen, the elixir of life is one of the best blood purifiers and one of the most effective nerve tonics that can be found in natural medicine. It is freely provided by nature to all, and will bring a new strength, vitality and a sense of pure happiness and positive attitude into your life.

Improper breathing and waste matter thrown off by the lungs causes retardation in digestion, skin problems, mental congestion, confusion of thought, and heart depression. The entire system becomes inactive and very susceptible to dis-ease. So…..synergize your breath daily for vitality and optimal wellness,

Enhance Your Ritual Experience

Set the mood by lighting a candle and your favorite potpourri in a simmering pot, or you may want to utilize essential oils such as frankincense and myrrh, jasmine, lavender or sandalwood in an oil diffuser. Invest in a Mood-lite- lighting system or lamp that offers color therapy. The Mood-lite absolutely changes the ambiance of a room. I put it in a lamp behind my comfortable massage chair, where I like to relax after everyone is in bed. I turn on my tableside waterfall and with my mood-lite softly glowing, I can truly relax and become 'stress free' after a long day. It creates a very serene atmosphere for relaxing and refreshes and rejuvenates the soul.

Mood-Scent Directions: *Add a small amount of the Mood-Scent to the groove in an aroma-ring and place firmly on the*

light bulb. Turn on the Mood-lite and soon the heat from the Mood-lite will evaporate the Mood-scent, infusing the scent of your choice into the air. The aroma-ring fits any standard size light bulb. Caution: Let Aroma-Ring cool before removing from the Mood-lite. www.mood-lites.com

Purchase lavender, yellow or blue light bulb for the lamp and create a color healing environment for this ritual. Now, you are ready to experience your synergy music massage for stress release, inner peace & serenity.

Relax yourself as much as you can and close your eyes gently. Inhale , slowly counting 1..2..3..4..5..etc., exhale using the same count 1..2..3..4..5…etc. Repeat this exercise at least 10 times. Pay close attention to the sensations in your body and you will notice a sense of calmness engulfing you as you allow your body to experience the deep relaxation that deep breathing creates.

SYNERGY MOVEMENTS

Synergy movements involve coordinating the many elements of BODY, MIND and SPIRIT so that they move simultaneously. While listening to synergy music, use the following movement suggestions and create your own Soul Dance. Synergy Music…..encourages rhythmic movements for increased stress release and inner peace. Synergy Music is a revolutionary rediscovery in the laws of physics, which indicates that our bodies resonate to sound. Harmonious music vibrations can stimulate the body to release stress, emotional energy and encourage feelings of happiness and joy. Gently close your eyes and concentrate upon each musical note until you find your body flowing with the symphonic melodies of the music. The following instructions guide you into a total synergy movement experience.

1. Leg and hip movements. Lift your legs and move your hips in a circle, from side to side, front and back, while lying on your back.

2. Shrug your shoulders upwards, downward and circles lift your arms above your head and circle your hands to the left and right. (keep your hand movements soft and light)

3. With your knees locked, slowly bend the spine by bending over slowly with your arms hanging downward towards the floor. (This helps to release back and shoulder tension)

4. Lift your arms outward to your sides. Begin rotating your arms in both directions

5. Let go of muscular volition and practice letting go of body mental control. Let the music inspire movement.

6. Toes and feet (point and swirl)

7. Gentle knee, joint movements (While sitting or laying on the floor)

8. Body joint movement

9. Deep breathing

10. Head rolls (in both directions)

11. Be creative and allow your own natural movements to guide you.

Don't forget to do lots of facial smiling and feeling a sense of inner peace.

With practice you will notice that these movements become a dance as your mind and spirit take off like the wind blowing effortlessly with the sounds of music.

As the physical body becomes uneasy,
your mental body will become uneasy…
so let go and synergize…………

The following illustrations give instructions on how to start your synergy movement meditation ritual. Remember, this takes time to realize benefits and requires daily practice. Movement of the energy centers is the key to increased energy, stress release and inner peace.

As the physical body becomes uneasy,

your mental body will become uneasy…

so let go and Synergize.

Synergy Movement Exercises

Relieving Neck Tension

Roll your head slowly to the left. Concentrate on stretching the muscles as you rotate around 5 times. Reverse the motion to the right. Concentrate on breathing freely taking a deep breath through the nose at the end of the fifth roll...... hold the breath for 5 seconds and then release slowly through your nose.

The Morning Stretch

You can do this exercise in the bed or on the floor. Lie on your back with your arms out at shoulder level, palms up, the backs of the wrists held firmly down on the floor. Bend your knees and bring them up as high as you can. Slowly roll them over from side to side, passing them as close to your chest as possible. Inhale while raising your knees up....and then exhale while bringing your knees down to the count of five. Remember to breathe correctly.

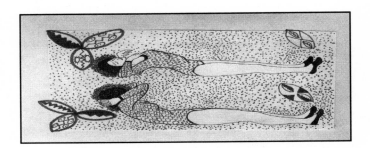

Relieving Neck Pain

Lie on your back. Bend your elbows, lift them a little higher than your shoulders, and push them against the floor or mattress hard enough to raise your chest off of the floor. As you do this, press the back holding your chest up high by leaning on your elbows and the back of your head. Hold this position for a few seconds, and then return to a straight flat position.

Follow the previous movement by clasping your hands behind your head and lifting it forward as high as you can. Let the head remain passive, and lift it by pulling it up with your hands. This will help reduce pain in the neck and teach you to create a more relaxed position for the head and shoulders.

The round image picture was designed by Ron "Iceman" Wallace

Relax Tired Legs, Feet, Lower Back

Begin by taking deep breaths to the count of five for 10 rounds....Then begin the synergy movement once you find a rhythmic flow, allow your mind to visualize your dreams and aspirations as a full reality! If you have varicose veins, this will help to reduce to the development of a more critical condition.

Lie on your back with your legs up against the wall. Keep your knees straight, and do as many foot exercises as you wish.

Flex your right foot while pointing your left foot and then reverse.

Spread your feet apart and then bring them together at the toes.

Flex your feet while rotating right foot backward ...left foot frontward. Be creative.

Total Relief of Back Tension

Do this exercise in a straight backed chair. Let yourself drop loosely forward until your hands rest on the floor. Slowly roll up; lifting your midsection first, as if someone took you by the waist to pull your back up. When you are all the way up, press the small of your back firmly against the chair back and stretch your arms up, without letting your back arch. This will help correct swayback, and alleviate the kind of lower back pain caused by poor posture or sitting still for long periods of time.

Visualize positive energy flowing through your hands. Inhale up...exhale down, concentrating on spinal energy centers releasing tension and pain.

Reliving Lower Back Tension

This exercise will help relive tension in the lower back area. With your feet apart, place your hands on your knees and push them apart as you bend loosely forward, letting your head hang down. Push your knees straight by leaning your hands on them and straightening the elbow. At the same time, lift your head and flatten your back until you are leaning out at right angles with the knees straight.

Concentrate on your lower back, knees, ankles, head and rectum energy centers. Before you focus on those areas, first begin to release the spinal energy centers from the top to the bottom. Inhale up and exhale down.

"It is well with my soul"

Inner Peace Movement

Inner Peace in the midst of a storm focuses on the neck and head energy centers. This helps neck tension and lengthens neck muscles shortened by poor head posture. Lie on you back. Your entire back and shoulders should be in contact with the bed or floor. Stretch your neck till it is as long as you can make it. Roll your head sideways until you can press your ear down to the bed. Keep rolling from side to side. Do not let the neck shorten.

Breathe deeply as you roll your head up and exhale fully as you roll your head down. Pause 10 seconds between each movement.

*Movement stimulates the nerves
and helps keep the spine flexible*

Daily Stretch Exercise Program

SYNERGY MOVEMENT-THE BODY TWIST- THE MINDFUL ROLL-THE HEALING ROCK
Derived from the Yoga Instructor Priestess Nura Dina-May God be with you wherever you are my sister

The Sunrise Stretch Ritual
(Synergy Movement)

When you first become aware that you have awakened to a new day, give thanks to the Creator for breath and life and a conscious mind. Remain in the bed and inhale deeply several breaths, take time to just be in the presence of self and God. Allow your mind to gently notice your body limb by limb, energy center by energy center and become aware of how you feel. Notice if you are experiencing any blockages or if you are feeling a total sense of peace and readiness for the day.... Make a decision that you are ready and prepare yourself to Synergize with breathing and stretching. Turn on your synergy music and begin to move with the music.

Breathing and Stretching

Gently inhale and exhale a few stomach breaths, and slowly move into a few good deep stretches. The following instructions will guide you into an effective stretch:

- stretch your hands above your head

- interlock your fingers with your palms turned out

- flatten your lower back on the bed or floor

- if you are standing or sitting up, move your arms and hands from side to side

- stretch your legs, arms and point your toes

- deeply inhale and exhale to the count of five 10-15 times

This movement is called the sunrise rejuvenating movement with breath

The Body Twist

Pull your knees to your chest and arms to your side with palms down. Drop your hips to one side (start to your left and then right) while back and shoulders remain on the floor. When twisting to the left face your head to the right. When twisting to the right, face your head to the left. This is good for twisting the spine energy centers and lower back. Do this movement slowly with your full attention on the body response to the stretch.

The Mindfull Roll

Pull your knees to your chest while lying on your back on a yoga floor mat. Embrace your knees and interlock your fingers to hold your knees in place. Roll from side to side on to the shoulder. This stretches the upper back energy center and neck energy center between the two shoulder blades. Repeat four times for grounding.

The Healing Rock

This movement appears to be difficult. Get that thought out of your mind and realize that it is simple and wonderful to accomplish.

Movement one - bring your knees to your chest

Movement two - cross your ankles

Movement three - grab your big toe or whatever is comfortable (HOLD TIGHT)

Movement four - rock up and down like a rocking horse.

This morning ritual will help to keep your mind focused and ready for a productive and peaceful day. It also serves as the inspiration to get up with readiness to practice your **S**ynergy **M**ovement **S**ound **M**editation.

CHAPTER THREE

Accessing the Higher Self

Connection with the Divine Mind

My Daily Meditation
and Prayer Ritual

PLACE YOUR NAME HERE

*WAKE UP GIVING THANKS AND PRAISE TO THE
CREATOR FOR LIFE*

*INSPIRATIONAL READING....(5 minutes)
MEDITATION AND THE BREATH......(15minutes)
A E I O U ~ (Mono tone Chant).....(5 minutes)
RECITE THE LORDS PRAYER
CLOSING*

Closing your Daily Meditation and Prayer Ritual should be different every day. Pay attention to your thoughts and inner voice during your morning ritual and notice a message gifted to you by the creator for that day. Allow a closing ritual to come to your mind and follow it.

Meditation....the inner accent....Divine......
Reality....the discipline of prayer, contemplation
and meditation are the means by which one ascends
through ever expanding and ever more refined spheres
of consciousness. To a state of union with the godhead
that lies at the core of his being. Healing dynamic
balance...chakras sacred energy centers..... are the
gateways of consciousness.......mental, astral and
etheric matter. Soul......on a higher mental plane,
good health depends on correct functioning of the
etheric body...the spiritual self.........Selah

Daily Prayer RITUAL
The Lord's Prayer

Our father which art in heaven, hollowed be they name.

Thy kingdom come, thy will be done

On earth as it is in heaven.

Give us this day, our daily bread.

And forgive us our debts, as we forgive our debtors.

And lead us not into temptation,

but deliver us from evil.

For thine is the kingdom and the

power and the glory, forever.

AMEN ~RA

The Deeper Meaning of The Lords Prayer

The Great Prayer is a comprehensive formula for the development and transformation of the soul. It is designed with the uttermost care for that specific purpose, so that those who use it regularly, with understanding, will experience a real change of soul/mind.

The more we analyze the LORDS PRAYER, The more wonderful its construction seems to be to me. It meets everyone's need no matter what religious affiliation one might be. The Lord's Prayer is one of my favorite songs to sing in the ***Sacred Symphonies Concert Tour***. I am always reminded of the great power of this prayer in song after I sing the last note. The audience is suddenly in a silent awe of the powerful tones and significant meaning of the words in the prayer. This song has the capacity to allow a divine tuning to occur with God's frequency of light and love. As the song comes to its crescendo, I can feel the energy of each listener's anticipation of the next note leading to the glorious poetic phrase and ultimate emotional release at the heart level, "For Thine is the Kingdom and the Power and the Glory Forever......................Amen".

Amen is the ultimate acknowledgment of omnipotence, and spiritual significance of The Kingdom of God's Reign.

The "Kingdom of God" means primarily the rule of God, the divine kingly authority of life on earth. The total sense of each line in the prayer is spiritually connected to the energy centers (chakras) of the body.

The Lord's Prayer and the energy centers of the human body are directly correlated to the chakra system. The chakra system represents the endocrine system, the body temple. The endocrine system of the human body regulates hormones which rule the emotions. The Chakra system can be connected to the great prayer gland by gland of the endocrine system. According to the Edgar Casey study of the Chakras, the following interpretation was developed of the Lord's Prayer.

Pituitary Center- Our father which art in Heaven/and the glory forever.

Pineal Center – Hollowed be thy name.

Thyroid Center- Thy kingdom come thy will be done/for thine is the kingdom.

Thymus Center – But deliver us from evil.

Adrenal Center – And forgive us our debts as we forgive our debtors.

Solar Plexus – And lead us not into temptation.

Gonad Center- Give us this day our daily bread.

This concept means that the prayer could be understood as a benefit to the physical and mental aspects of ourselves, especially when we contemplate the flow of meaning for each verse.

Understanding Soul Language, its influence in our lives, and how it brings the mind/body/spirit, the tri-consciousness, into greater harmony, moves us even closer to the final objective of inner peace and emotional balance.

Jesus foresaw that as the centuries went by; his simple, primitive teaching would slowly become overburdened, and misinterpreted by all sorts of external things which really have nothing what so ever to do with the prayer. He foresaw that men who had never known him, relying, seriously, upon their own limited intellects, would build up theologies doctrinal systems, obscuring the direct simplicity of his spiritual message.

The first thing that we notice is that the Prayer naturally falls into seven clauses. Seven symbolizes individual completeness, the perfection of the individual soul, the epitome of personal transformation. God created the heavens and the earth in seven days. There is also an eighth clause added – Thine is the kingdom, the power, and the glory. This phrase in itself is an excellent affirmation.

All seven parts contain everything that we need to nourish the soul. From the mind, to the heart, to the universe, to the ultimate affirmation that our experience on earth be that of an experience in heaven; which implies that heaven is on earth. The prayer pleads with God to feed our spirits everyday with the bread of life. The "Bread of Life" is the spiritual food needed by man/woman. Without the bread of life man cannot live spiritually. The bread of life is universal truth and knowledge. In order to understand if there is any such thing as absolute truth / universal truth, let us first begin by defining what truth is. Truth is defined by the dictionary as "conformity to fact or actuality; a statement proven to be or accepted as true; reality or actuality." Some people today would say that there is no true reality, only perceptions and opinions. On the other hand, others would argue that there must be some absolute reality or truth somewhere. The existence of absolute truth / universal truth can be found embedded in the existence of religion. All the religions of the world are an attempt to give meaning and definition to life. They are born out of the fact that mankind desires something more than simply existing. Behind all religion, is a fundamental belief that there must be more to life than simply this physical existence that we now know. Through religion, people are looking for assurance and hope for the future, for forgiveness of sins, for peace in the midst of our struggles, and for answers to our deepest questions. Religion is really evidence that mankind is more than simply a highly evolved entity. It is evidence of a higher purpose, and the fact that there is indeed a personal and purposeful Creator, who implanted into man the desire to seek knowing GOD. If indeed there is a Creator, then GOD becomes the standard for absolute truth, and it is GOD's authority that establishes that truth. In the context of the meaning of GOD, let us consider GOD as the spirit of Light in the form of man for the purpose of manifestation.

Just as physically the human being needs to eat in order to live, the bread of life gives nourishment for the soul. Unless one eats from the bread of life, the ultimate experience is eternal death. The Great Prayer is a daily reminder to contemplate and concentrate on the power of forgiveness, and not to allow feelings of anger, mistrust, or emotional pain from the past to impede upon your day to day existence in the moment. The great prayer is an armor of protection from the tendency to do things that we know we should not do. This Great Prayer is the ultimate confession of a spiritual power over all existence, which solely resides in the heart of man.

Let Us Pray...Meditation & Chant

And now it is time for meditation and reflection on the word of god.

Listen to my voice as I take you on a journey of inner peace and enlightenment.

Take a deep breath...inhale deeply the love of God...and exhale the inner peace of God...inhale and release... ...focus your attention on the breath....As you allow your mind to rest upon the power of the creator ...give ear to my words, o lord, consider my meditation....my inspiration.

Hearken unto the voice of my cry...... my mother, father, and God...........for unto thee I will pray. And now slowly close your .... eyes...and take three more deep cleansing breaths and then open your eyes slowly, blinking them several times before opening completely.

(Repeat this prayer out loud)
OUR FATHER, MOTHER, GOD....THOU ART LIFE AND HELP AND JOY AND PEACE, AND ONLY AS I MANIFEST-MANIFEST THESE IN MY DAILY LIFE...MAY I ENJOY PEACE OF MIND...INNER PEACE OF THOUGHT

GIVE OH MOTHER, FATHER, GOD THAT PEACE,

THAT JOY, THAT LOVE TO ME O LORD…..
CREATE IN ME A PURE HEART AND RENEW THE
RIGHTEOUS SPIRIT WITHIN ME…CLEANSING
MY LIFE, MY HEART, MY BODY, THROUGH THE
LOVE IN THE CHRIST CONSCIOUNESS OF MY
SOUL..

LET PEACE AND HARMONY REIGN WITHIN MY
BODY…MY MIND..MY SOUL……

PRAISE YE THE LORD…PRASIE YE THE LORD
FROM THE HEAVENS WITHIN…PRAISE THE
GOD PRESENCE WITHIN EACH MIND AND
HEART.

PRAISE YE HIM, ALL HIS ANGELS

PRAISE YE HIM, ALL HIS ASCENDED MASTERS

PRAISE YE HIM, THE SUN AND THE MOON AND
THE STARS

THE GREAT AFRICAN ANCESTORSSSSS

PRAISE HIM, YE HEAVENS, AND
YE WATERS AND THE ANGELS OF
PROTECTIONNNNNNNNNNN

PRAISE YE HIM FOR VITALITY, THE KUNDALINI

LIFE FORCE ENERGY...... (Chant) LAM (visualize the color RED)

PRAISE YE HIM FOR CREATIVY, RESERVED SEXUAL ENERGY....(chant) VAM (visualize the color ORANGE)

PRAISE YE HIM FOR INSPIRATION, WISDOM AND INTELLECT.....(chant) RAM (visualize the color YELLOW)

GIVE THANKS AND PRAISE FOR LOVE/ HEALING/ BALANCE......(chant) YAM (visualize the color GREEN)

GIVE THANKS AND PRAISE FOR CLAIRAUDIENCE, RELAXATION......(chant) HAM (visualize the color BLUE)

GIVE THANKS AND PRAISE FOR THE VISION OF THE THIRD EYE...SPIRITUALITY... (Chant) AUM (visualize the color INDIGO)

CHRIST CONSCIOUSNESS...CHRIST CONSCIOUNESS INSPIRATION...... (Chant) OMMMMMMMM (visualize the color VIOLET)

REMEMBER THAT PART OF THE SOUL.. LINKED TO ALL THINGS... LINKED TO OUR TRUE SPIRITUAL ESSENCE..... (Chant)

OMMMMMMMMMMMMMMM (visualize the color PURPLE)

LET EVERYTHING THAT HATH BREATH PRAISE THE LORD

LET EVERYONE THAT HATH ENLIGHTENMENT SPREAD THE WORD…

*What you hold in your mind is
what you tend to experience*

Sound Healing With Sound Vibronics™

How To Fine-Tune and Get The Best Performance From Your Human Instrument The Body Temple

Current research proves that sound frequencies can literally relieve stress, lower blood pressure, improve tissue and cellular structure of the body and help manage emotional and physical pain. Sound Vibronics™ carries the power of sonic frequencies to heal the body, strengthen the mind and unlock hidden traumas and fears from the past that hold us back in life at the bio ~ energetic level. We can use Sound Vibronics, ™ universal and self-generated tones to help us become more sensitive to our rhythms and cycles of life. Sound and vibration influences mental and emotional states, spiritual awareness and the physical body. When the emotions have become frozen due to stressful events or traumas, sound and musical frequency interventions may coax painful emotions out of their hiding places in the psyche and physical body, into a place of healing and emotional balance. For individuals that are caught in the grip of unyielding sorrow or barely suppressed rage, sound can foster an unexpected equilibrium after a long period of distress.

Sound offers a profound relaxation response for emotional

and physical wellness. Studies and clinical observation suggest that sound interventions elicit the "relaxation Response", the term coined by cardiologist Herbert Benson, M.D. This relaxation response encourages our capacity to counteract the body's fight-or flight stress response.

How To Achieve A State Of Inner Balance

Inner healing is achieved when the Brain State reaches Alpha and Theta levels of functioning. The Vibrational tones of Sound Vibronics™ can induce these states of brain functioning instantly. Alpha is a mind state of external awareness and Theta is an inward directed state of awareness, an inner reality experienced as real, such as images during meditation or visualization. The healing is experienced when the Brain State reaches Alpha or Theta; the ego is given permission to release control. The body has the capacity to heal itself when offered the correct conditions with sound frequencies; this includes the sound inward and outward of prayer. Prayer thoughts are translated into sound frequencies that send intentional messages into the cosmos. The Brain State is an ancient tool for going inward to create a connection with the nervous system and decrease muscle tension, respiration and negative stress levels in the body. Edgar Casey made a prophetic statement when he said that "sound will be the medicine of the future".

OUR MIND REGULATES ITS ACTIVITY BY MEANS OF ELECTRIC WAVES WHICH ARE REGISTERED IN THE BRAIN, EMITTING TINY ELECTOCHEMICAL IMPULSES OF VARIED FREQUENCIES, WHICH CAN BE REGISTERED. THESE BRAIN WAVES ARE KNOWN AS:

BETA Brain Waves (13-30 cycles per second)

Is the fastest state of consciousness, representing the most intense state of alertness. The result of this brain state is an intense state of alertness. The *Sensorium Method*™ teaches how to tune this state for maximum mind power.

ALPHA Brain Waves (8 to 12 cycles per second)

This brain wave indicates a relaxed state of mind. A meditative mind set. It is a state of relaxed alertness, good for inspiration, learning facts fast. The left and right brain are working together. Alpha Brain waves are very effective for learning & creating mental clarity. Meditation teaches us how to connect with the Alpha state that serves as an antenna into inner peace and serenity.

THETA Brain Waves (4 to 8 cycles per second)

This is a state of deep meditation. This is associated with life-like imagination. The Theta Brain wave is a high state of mental concentration, highly sensitive with an increased intuitive mind state.

DELTA Brain Waves (0.5 to 4 cycles per second)

This Brain wave is a state of deep dreamless sleep.

The brain is a powerful tool…it pays to learn how to use it. The human mind has infinite power and it is you're most fundamental resource for attaining serenity and inner peace. Learning about brain wave functioning can certainly expand your mind power, memory retention, health and awareness.

Achieving Inner Balance with Vibrational Healing

Vibrational Healing is often described as healing through the use of sound with voice, animated instruments like the crystal quarts singing bowls, drum, harp, wind and string instruments. The sounds that are used in a healing session induce a shift in consciousness which helps one to get unstuck from beliefs in disease, misfortune, pain etc. Actually, it is not the sound; it is the no-tone between tones that has a healing effect. It is the silence that takes us back to our pure state of being. Silence…this is not the absence of sound, it is the distant residue of sound (just like space is the distant residue of matter). Silence helps to quiet mental chatter that is distracting from the inner voice of God. It is this voice that has the answers to all of our desires and needs.

Inner Sound is healing through the use of silence......get still and hear your inner sounds and find the inner answers that you seek in life. The singing quartz crystal bowls are a source of deeply profound vibrational medicine, which leads one into a powerful state of meditated silence. After a session with the singing crystal bowls, there is a period of silence that takes you into a place of perfect peace, which feels like you have just visited heaven and heard the profound voice of God and the presence of angels. This experience substantiates that everything in the universe is in a state of vibration, and the resonance created by the crystal vibration can be experienced by all as a deeply penetrating waves of healing energy and source of inner peace. The singing crystal bowl vibrations emit a pure state of radiant light and sound which corresponds with the vibration of the etheric body. It is the etheric body that requires cleansing and strengthening during periods of dis-stress, which then allows the physical and etheric body to heal. Each crystal bowl is made of 99.8% silicon quartz. The quartz crystal bowl sound and vibration penetrates the human body, and creates a deep sense of awareness and healing. The human body is composed of water and crystallite substances that respond to high frequency levels of sound as vibrational medicine. The human bone structure, DNA and even blood are biological components of liquid crystalline structures. When dis-ease and dis-stress begin to penetrate the body, the fluidic system of body secretions become toxic and can form into hard crystalline deposits, blocking the flow of life energy. The Vibrational frequencies of crystal resonance can emit high levels of brain wave activity creating altered states of consciousness, allowing the body to reach deep levels of relaxation. Consistent levels of deep relaxation encourage optimal wellness and dis-ease prevention. This highly electromagnetic state of consciousness can actually penetrate bio-photons, breaking up and dissolving toxic blockages in the psychical and etheric body. This high level of electromagnetic energy can result into experiences of deep, deep relaxation in seconds, reducing stress instantaneously. This level of vibrational medicine can increase blood flow, enhance the immune response and fully integrate mind and body, transcending into higher levels of consciousness.

A Very wonderfully vibrational healing Tea Toddy was given to me by my sister Nataska Hummingbird that is a great combination with vibrational healing rituals. The Healing Tea Toddy is called Sequoia's Delight.

To make this healing toddy, you will need the raw herbs to make your own tea bag or steeping combination for a tea ball.

Sequoia's Delight –Herbal Hot Tea Toddy

4 teaspoons of nettle

3 teaspoons of alfalfa

4 teaspoons of horse tail

6 teaspoons of oats straw

4 teaspoons of mother's wart

Boil 5 quarts of water and then cut off the heat source. Pour the raw herbs into a strainer and let steep on top of the stove for 15 minutes, no longer than 20 minutes. Pour yourself a cup of tea and sweeten it with honey, no sugar please. And enjoy your Sequoia's Delight. Thank you Hummingbird, for **Sequoia's herbal** healing combination. May God Bless Mountain Eagle Place.

Toning for Inner Healing

The Webster's Ninth New Collegiate Dictionary defines tone as "an act of stretching, vocal or musical sound of a specific quality". Toning is creating a sense of healthy elasticity within the structure of any stimulus. Toning creates stimuli by vibrating sensory organs in the body, evoking muscular contraction and glandular secretion. By stimulating glandular secretions, the vibration and sounds help to create a healthy process for the body to experience optimal health. Toning allows the voice and body to work in harmony, creating a particular inflection of sound for inner peace and emotional balance. Intentionally directed sound from the diaphragm to the vocal chords, establishes a correct environmental influence for creating a state of physical and mental equilibrium. Sound vibration from toning aligns the mind, physical body and spirit with potential healing.

Toning encourages the thought processes and the physical body to release emotional stress and mental congestion. Effective toning for longs periods of time has the power to create an electrical response in the body, increasing the internal vibratory rate of each cell, organ and muscle. It may even be possible to physically move blockages in the body system with sound vibration. It may equally be possible to influence mental awareness and life outcomes with sound vibration, intention and thought. The walls of the nervous system and blood vessels are fine tuned with toning, thus creating a mental expansion for increased memory, stress release and inner peace.

The Healing Benefits of Toning

1. Toning synchronizes and balances brainwaves within a few moments.

2. Toning reduces stress and releases negative emotion.

3. Toning internally vibrates and massages your body.

4. Toning improves health.

5. Toning empowers the speaking voice.

6. Toning improves listening abilities.

7. Toning releases tension instantly.

8. Toning improves self-esteem.

9. Toning balances hemispheres of the brain allowing the integration of left and right brain functions. Producing a more creative awareness of life.

10. Toning can slow down the aging process.

What is toning?

Toning is achieved through the elongation of a musical note or tone, using the breath and the voice. Toning is the universal soul language of sound and vibration. It encourages the bio-energetic field by assisting in the release of old patterns of emotional, physical and mental limitations, allowing you to experience emotional freedom and spiritual enlightenment.

What is Sound?

Sound is a vibration or wave of air molecules cause by the motion of an object. A sound wave contains energy, which in turn means it can make things move. Sound energy can be changed into other forms of energy such as electricity or light. Sound can change other forms of matter with mental intent and verbal suggestion. Sound can translate into visual mental images with color. Sound is Pure Vibration. The Chakra system responds to sound and has the capacity for balancing and restoring the endocrine system. Light is faster than sound and thought is faster than light. Therefore, the synergistic movement of thought (intention), light and sound = manifest, manifest, manifest into reality. This is a very powerful concept to contemplate. If our thoughts are faster than light and sound, imagine what levels of vibrational frequencies that we could create just with our thoughts, coupled with the visualization of light and the audible experience of sound waves. The possibility for manifest is increased tenfold. Therefore, it is critical that our thoughts are carefully developed to create only that which we desire to manifest in our lives. The mind is electro magnetism in its highest form of matter. When matter or form meets with light, God is manifested into life. Should all of humanity create a focused attention on the highest attributes and thoughts of love, the love vibration would have universal permission to pour down from the heavens upon the earth as if a gigantic magnet was pulling with great force streams of light from the cosmos, simultaneously from all directions throughout the universe. Creating cosmotic love vibrations for healing of self, the world and the earth is critical, and must be practiced on a daily basis by all of humanity. Cosmotic Love Vibrations......are awaiting your permission to flow.........

Remember Love

TONING Ritual for Inner Healing

The following chart is your guide to musical keynotes that can be used while toning for inner healing. You can use the keyboard to determine the key that you should tone or chant in. If you do not have a keyboard, you can purchase a chromatic pitch instrument from your local music store. I recommend the Master Key Pitch instrument made by WM. KRATT CO USA.

In the Key of F repeat the following word, Ayare'sa. Ayare'sa means, inner healing, in the West African language TWI.

Ayare'sa….Ayare'sa….Ayare'sa. Focus your attention on the center of your forehead and visualize the word Ayare'sa in the silence in the key of F in your mind.

Now close your eyes and take three deep breaths, repeat the word Ayre'sa in the key of F, while in the silence, repeat this word up to ten times, creating a mantra for your daily meditation. Mantra is a Sanskrit word which literally means "a tool of thought". In various meditation traditions, a mantra is used for focus and concentration. The mantra is a word that is focused on to assist one with attaining mental clarity and focus. The mantra assists with quieting the mind. The mantra has the capacity to transform consciousness. The mantra is intended to offer a rhythmic sound pattern that is repeated in your mind on the inhale of the breath and the second part of the mantra is repeated on the exhale of the breath. So for example the meditation with the mantra would go like this;

Inhale breath and mentally repreat, "Ayare" exhale "sa", with attention on the center of your forehead. It is as if you are visualizing the word in writing in your mind's eye located just above your eye brows in the center of your forehead. Your mantra is a very personal sound. It can be any sound or phrase that you feel comfortable with. Meditation is not a religion; it is a scientific practice that has proven to serve as a catalyst for improved health, mental clarity, increased memory and over all optimal health.

MUSICAL *KEYNOTES TO LIFE*

Life Key Note	Chakra	Gland	Soul Personality
B	CROWN	PINEAL	SPIRITUALITY
A	THIRD EYE	PITUITARY	INTUITION
G	THROAT	THYROID	EXPRESSING THE WILL
F	HEART CHAKRA	THYMUS	HUMANITY
E	SOLAR PLEXUS	PANCREAS	PERSONAL POWER
D	SACRAL CHAKRA	REPRODUCTIVE ORGANS	SENSATIONS
C	ROOT CHAKRA	ADRENAL GLAND	SURVIVAL

Sound Vibronics Toning Ritual

START WITH HUMMING…...in the silence or with instrumental music playing in the background.

Begin to

MOVE YOUR HEAD FROM RIGHT TO LEFT HUMMING

MOVE HANDS SLOWLY UP AND DOWN WHILE
HUMMING

Slowly Shift to

Chant:

A… E…. I…. O….. U

OM -EEEEE

OM-AHHHHHH

AH LEY LUOO YAAAA

OM…… EEEEEEEE…………..

EEEE-OM

TAKE STATEMENTS FROM WORLD RELIGIONS
AND CULTURES. PUT THEM TO MUSIC
AND RECITE THEM OUTLOUD. ENJOY THE
VIBRATIONS OF THE WORDS AND MUSIC,
WHILE YOU ARE HAVING A GREAT TIME IN
SOUND FOR HEALING. And so it is. And so it shall
be….

Listen With Your Heart in the Silence

CHAPTER FOUR

Emotional Wellness

A Movement Meditation for Forgiveness

...Take three deep breaths

Focus your mind on your intention for forgiveness

ACT WITH NO RESISTANCE

(Sit in a comfortable position, with your spine straight and shoulders back)

Step # One: Begin to move your right arm slowly upwards towards the sky, taking a deep breath through the nose.

Step # Two: Begin to move your left arm upwards towards the sky during the first breath upwards. (Hold your breath to count of five)

Step # Three: Touch the tips of both fingers together over your head, and begin to bring your arms down simultaneously, while exhaling through your mouth. (Expel of the air)

Step # Four: Rest both hands on your lap with your palms facing upwards.

Step # Five: Repeat steps # one thru four seven times

Repeat the following affirmation in a mono tone out loud:

I forgive myself

I forgive all relationships current & from the past that have caused me grief

All past relations i forgive

I forgive the world & call for world peace

I forgive my family, my mother, my father, my uncle, my aunt etc._____.

I forgive everyone that i belive have ever hurt me

I now forgive myself for any grief, harm, hurt or pain that i have held on to up until this very moment in my life. I release it once and for all!!!!!!

Oh…..that sounds so wonderful!!!!!! I release it and let it go once and for all. I am reading this passage during my final edits of the book, and I am aware that I have written this book for myself. In this very moment, I am in need of this Forgiveness Ritual. As I opened my mouth to repeat the last line of this passage, I was suddenly struck into an awe of realization that I must forgive right now, once and for all. I stopped dead in my tracks and became stuck with the idea of giving up the pain, the hurt, the disappointment, the grief, and the harm. It would seem to make since that one would want to release these awful emotions, however, I am right now in this very moment aware that somewhere deep inside of me does not want to submit to letting go. I want to blame and insist that the source of what I believe my grief and pain is all about must first come correct with me and my life and the world. I want them to tell the world how terrible they are and what disgust they have for themselves and offer a lifetime of income and apologies to me for their acts of hurt and pain. I am aware of how easily said and not so easy to do. I am also aware that it is my responsibility to do the healing work for myself. It is not easy to accept and realize that the hurt, pain and grief that I feel are all about me, and my willingness to change. Do I love myself enough to let go of the repeating patterns that leave me in a state of pure overwhelming sorrow? However, it is a simple process of allowing the hurt, pain and grief to have its moment of glory, and then release it into the universe forever, once and for all, and I choose to let it go, let it flow like a river.

AMEN

Practice Playing Your Key Notes to Life

The Miracles Ritual

Repeat after me, "I am looking for great things to happen in my life right now! This is the year that all things hoped for will manifest, manifest, manifest. I am ready for my miracles."

What miracles are you expecting? Are you being still enough or even faithful enough to know? Well, if you are or if you are not, get ready for the formula. From this day forward you will not miss your miracles. Universal law helps us to know that Universal life force is impartial and unemotional; it is pure energy. Whatever thoughts, feelings or actions we project are reflected back to us in the form of our daily experiences. In our thinking, we must first find a way to unlock the lack that we have learned and release it to receive miracles in our lives. All things are possible – good health, wealth, creativity and spiritual growth. If you just believe without a shadow of a doubt, your mind will take you there.

Did you know that you are not your body, your emotions or any of the social, cultural or religious restrictions that you have been taught to be? You are an infinite part of the Universal life force in physical form allowing you to develop spiritually, focusing on soul purpose. Your mind does not know this, it wants to rationalize and create logic for you. Operating logically is death to the creative miracle maker in you. The power is within you and you must realize its presence. Before you begin to create a miracle blue print, you must, meditate and focus on what it is you are attempting to create. The key here is not to limit your thinking, remember all things are possible and the outcome is whatever God's will is, with your action. Any contradictory thought patterns will confuse the Universal life force energy, therefore you must practice having absolute pure thoughts and good intentions. If a negative contradiction comes up, cancel it immediately. The **Miracle Blue Print Plan** begins in your personal daily journal located at the end of this book. Write down all of the things your heart desires. Those things that you need to manifest to fulfill your soul's purpose, or even to discover your soul's purpose.

Be sure to be clear and exact in your
plan by using specific detail.

Now this is the miracle ritual process:

1. **Read your daily list** at least **twice a day.**
   Once in the morning and once at night.

2. **Meditate on your hearts desires**, knowing that in your heart you are just waiting for the manifestation.

3. **Do not share these thoughts**, keep them to yourself. Thoughts are energy and everyone that you think is in your corner many not be. Keep it to yourself until your miracle happens.

4. **Have the state of mind** that you have already received your miracle and enjoy that mental state of mind.

5. **Realize that your miracles could come** from places unknown to you, so do not limit yourself to where your miracles will come from. Stay alert and see the power of God in everything that you do.

6. **Give thanks to the creator** for your blessings as they come and as they are forthcoming.

Inner peace and balance to you .... God Bless you .... be sure to be clear and exact in your plan by using specific detail. Practice this ritual when you need power in manifesting your desires in life.

This is your Debt Free Affirmation

Power of the Mind Ritual

Ask yourself this question

I wonder what it would be like to have no financial debt and an abundance of prosperity?

REPEAT OUT LOUD:

THERE IS NO DEBT IN THE DIVINE MIND

ABUNDANCE IS INFINITE. And so it is!

(Repeat out loud and in the silence as many times as you wish) Note from Ivy:

(Just know in your mind and heart that this is your true reality)

I accept infinite prosperity and abundance with a debt-free life.

AND SO IT IS…..... and so it shall be!

In your mind's eye (the third eye) visualize a debt free life. This includes financial and emotional debts owed in relationships with others, debt that you created for yourself, promises that you did not keep, projects that remain incomplete, etc. Once you have begun the visualization, begin to write down in your journal all of these debts that come to mind. For each of these debts repeat the debt free affirmation above as many times during the day as you remember for three days at a time. This ritual can also be done in meditation with a white candle and jasmine incense and synergy music. The Power of the Mind Ritual creates a new way of being and thinking each day. You are empowered by your own thoughts and feelings to trust your own inner power. With your thoughts and intention, you can create whatever truth you desire in your life. Everything begins with the mind, THE INNER VOICE, THE WORD and the universe will follow you.

Manifesting prosperity and abundance is the primary objective of the Power of the Mind Healing Ritual. Prosperity is the condition of being successful or thriving, especially in physical health and economic well-being.

To gain a clear understating of the science of manifesting prosperity and abundance, you must first have a understating of why Quantum physics is the key to the success of the Power of the Mind Healing Ritual. Science is finally admitting that everything in the universe is based on consciousness. As the observer of life, you are influencing what you are observing with your thoughts. This simply means that there is no objective reality, just the opposite of what we were all taught in school. For the first time in history, science is now able to provide the evidence of what mystics and enlightened individuals have claimed throughout the ages. "Your thoughts create reality and what you experience". Your ideas, beliefs and concepts are creating the world that you experience in life. This leads to the final conclusion that if you would like to change something in your life, you can by simply changing your thoughts, beliefs and concepts. Some call this the law of attraction, others call it the matrix, and I call it the power of Manifest! Manifest! Manifest! Use your thought frequencies and intense focus, to manifest your hearts deepest desires. This is the same principle of prayer power. With faith the size of a mustard seed, your prayers will manifest, manifest, manifest. That is as long as you avoid the consciousness of doubt. Creating reality with your thoughts is a fundamental ability of consciousness. This is why it is clearly critical that you pay attention to your thoughts at all times. Statistics on rich and successful people show that simply shifting their thinking was the major key that changed their lives. This could be associated with self esteem or self confidence in one's ability to create and manifest. Manifesting your dreams does not depend on your level of education; ethnicity or you're heritage. Most importantly, it is essential to realize that it doesn't even depend on your environment. It is clearly the result of your level of consciousness and what is dominating your thoughts. Direct you're thinking towards the reality that you want to create in life, and witness the manifestation of prosperity and abundance. Remember that success is not simply luck; it is the direct result of your ability to focus with intention, use your faith power and resist doubt. This is now a scientific proven fact. As you begin to practice the Debt Free Affirmation, remember to only allow thoughts into your consciousness that supports your desired outcome only. If any thoughts of doubt or disbelief try to creep into your mind, release it immediately and visualize your emotional and mental destination.

FAITH POWER

"Faith is the substance of things hoped for, the evidence of things not seen."

How many of us today operate on an absolute faith-based life? Do you think you do, or do you plan to in the near future? Faith does not question. Faith knows. So if you live your life based on faith, then you know you are on the path that reaches and dwells in God Power. Your inner God Power has the potential of accomplishing all the things that your soul desires. Faith is such a powerful level of consciousness. Know if you can conceive it, you can achieve it. Put it in your mind and watch it manifest based on the amount of Faith Power you possess.

Having a lack of faith means, disbelief, in the possibility of what you desire. Lack of faith means expected perpetual failure in any conscious use of planning for the future. If this sounds familiar to you, then maybe it is time to develop your Faith Power. Get above mental thoughts and their forces, and allow the One God to lead you, then you will not be misled. Faith Power is the key word for this ritual. Faith Power will lead you right to the doors of success in life and create a more peaceful, calm and assuring feeling inside.

So be still and know that you are that which you desire to be. Translate your dreams into being by using Faith Power and just imagine yourself already there. You have the power to become more than what and who you are, knowing faith does not question, faith knows.

If you are interested in building your faith power, contact Healing Temple of Light Sanctuary at www. serenityhealingsarts.com and learn how to create your own Spiritual Life Support Group.

Stay in the light of love......... share this one with a friend.

VISION'S...Meditation Ritual

A VISUALIZATION RITUAL FOR CREATING THE PERFECT LIVING AND WORK ENVIORNMENT

What is visualization?

Visualization is a mind-body practice where mental images are used to focus energy on relaxation, healing and manifesting. In visualization, individuals focus on a particular scene or situation with intent to relieve stress or receive healing or to create a sense of reality within the mind/body. Visualization can increase your ability to achieve goals, improve self confidence and build self esteem. Some alternative medicine practitioners use visualization with cancer patients attempting to relieve symptoms, or as an adjunct to cancer treatment. Visualization is essentially the process of mental imagery meditation. It's getting yourself into a deeply-relaxed state and then using your mind to create positive images of something you want to achieve, or manifest. Visualization is *"conscious creation"* by tapping the unlimited mind power of your brain. It's using the power you were born with to live life on purpose, rather than by chance. Visualization is a process that can be used to retrain the brain to create new images, beliefs and psycho-emotional responses in the body.

As individual beings, we create our own reality, consciously or unconsciously. It's our attitudes and beliefs that shape our experiences and dictate who and what we tend to draw into our lives. Like attracts the same. That is the Law of Attraction in action, and it's what we purposely create when we use the power of visualization to imagine something we desire.

Conscious Creation is excitingly empowering. Your creative mind power is capable of taking you wherever you want to go in life. Visualization is going deep within, and getting in touch with your inner mind, allowing images to manifest with clarity and power. It is almost like discovering an alternate world of reality. It's relaxing your mind and body and getting clear about what it is you want to manifest. Often that means first getting clear about what it is that you don't want in your life. This is an urgent warning; this technique is very powerful and it works, so get very clear during this process of what you really do not want to experience and clear it from your consciousness. Do the deep work of reaching a meditative state and imagining what you want as though it was already yours and you'll be amazed at what you can indeed accomplish.

Allow your source energy to do its thing. This is also a lesson on the power of prayer. Once you've visualized your goal and accepted it as yours, turn it over to the universe, like a prayer. That's how you tap into universal flow. Create your vision as real in your mind and then release it. By doing so, you're allowing the universe to support you.

Once you have released your visualization, start to take action doing what you can do to make it a reality in your physical world. Taking action and working hard is a useful lesson to learn in the process of visualization. However, it is just as important to learn to relax and meditate on things of your heart's desire, so that visualizing comes easy to manifest. Balancing hard work with relaxation is the passageway to joy, success and happiness in life.

Visualization balances the work that needs to be done.

It allows you to relax, replenish and re-energize, while keeping the vision alive and well. While in this meditative state, you will often feel the presence of universal life force energy pouring into your being. That's when you know that you've made the connection. The most important ingredient in the process of visualization is the critical reality of believing it to be so. You have to believe and be willing to act as though whatever you need is already on its way. Whatever you visualize is already happening in your feeling world. Mastering the skill of mental imagery can change your life in ways that you cannot even imagine.

The Visualization Ritual

Visualize the exact living and work environment that you see yourself in, within the next few months to one year. (write out your vision on paper and create a vision board with pictures detailing the exact images of your vision).

INSTRUCTIONS ON CREATING AN EFFECTIVE VISUALIZATION

Locate a quiet place where you will not be distracted by noise. Sit in a comfortable position, preferably with a straight back.

Always begin your visualization by quieting the mind

with 3 to 10 deep cleansing breaths. (Breathe deeply in through the nose and exhale through the mouth, filling your lungs completely with air and expanding the abdomen, contracting the abdomen with each exhale)

Focus your attention on the center of your forehead and allow the images to simply appear in the mind of your hearts deepest desires. It is very important that you do not allow your ego to take over your vision. Just allow the vision to appear after you ask yourself the question that you seek the answer to. This can be done in the silence or with very soft instrumental music. Begin to visualize your perfect living and work environment with no limitations or doubt. Remember there is no doubt in the DIVINE MIND. Abundance is infinite. Do not limit yourself with your inner disbelief in what you can or cannot achieve.

Practice this daily and begin to witness the changes in your life. Remember the key is to practice quieting the mind with meditation, visualize with great detail your intention, and then write out your vision on paper.

Grief, Loss and Healing

Grief shows up in our lives in many ways. It is not always associated with the death of a love one. Grief is an emotion that is connected to a mental, spiritual and or physical response. The mental response creates images and beliefs in the mind. The physical response is associated with how the emotions of grief manifest themselves literally in the physical body. The spiritual response is connected to faith, personal outcomes and ability to cope with loss. During a lifetime of experiences, we could encounter many traumatic and painful losses. Grief, trauma and loss could happen thousands, and maybe even millions of times in a lifetime. Each occurrence has its own identity, purpose and response. To become mentally and spiritually aware of the response is the passageway to resolving the grief and surviving it successfully. I use the word successful survival because I have witnessed grief and loss survivors that have not experienced it successfully. In the process of healing from suffering a loss, grief is inevitable. There are seven known stages within the grief and loss process. However, we now know that no one experiences grief in the same cyclic process as another. Therefore, I offer the following stages as points of reference and awareness of what to expect during a time of grief and the experience of loss.

The first stage of grief is *denial.* It is difficult for our minds to accept that such a loss has taken place in our lives. It is so much easier to cope with an idea of loss if we can believe that it did not really occur. The second stage of grief and loss is *anger.* In most cases we have no control over the loss that we experience, and thus react to our state of vulnerability with anger. This anger usually shows up as some type of aggression towards others or in a self blaming of the loss. The third stage is *guilt and bargaining.* We find ourselves trying to discover a way to reverse the outcome of the loss. This is a time when we begin to think about what could have been done to avoid the loss. It is not an unusual emotion to blame ourselves for something that we did or did not do to prevent the loss. Guilt can be associated with many types of losses such as the loss of a significant job, relationship or even death. We think of ways that we could do anything to turn back the hands of time. It is critical in the healing process to realize and accept the fact that there are events in life that we cannot control. Most likely, whatever the loss is, nothing could have been done to prevent it, you must find a way to forgive, release and move on. *Depression* is the fourth stage of grief and loss. This is a time when a great sense of hopelessness and maybe even guilt begin to take control of the emotions. Depression is an emotion that must be resolved before it reaches a level of uncontrollable intensity. If this stage of grief and loss is experienced for extended periods of time, professional help should be found to support the resolution of the depression. The fifth stage is *anxiety*. Fear and anxiety are natural emotions of grief. Physical symptoms of disturbance in sleeping patterns, panic, and feelings of being restless, fatigue, tearfulness and worry are common emotions during this time of grief. Anxiety can be painful and create other life disturbances if it is not resolved or managed quickly. Anxiety is an emotion that shows up when we are experiencing something that does not feel complete. Take care of the unfinished business and anxiety will eventually escape you. The sixth stage is *acceptance*. After the full range of emotions is experienced during the grief and loss process, one finally comes to a place of acceptance of the reality. Acceptance brings a total sense of release of guilt, responsibility, anger, denial and the need to bargain for change. The seventh stage is *Healing.* Finding freedom from the hold of grief and loss comes gradually in time. The amount of time that it takes to heal can depend on the type of loss and the overall circumstances of the individual's ability to cope. The time associated with grief is also connected to ones direct relationship to the loss. A very good example of this is the traumatic experience that the entire world witnessed on September 11, 2001, which later became known as the tragedy of 9-11. I was blessed to become one of the Clinical Social Workers appointed to work with the United Way response to the grief, loss and healing of victims who were personally and directly impacted by the aftermath of 9-11. This included survivors of family members and co-workers who had lost their lives at the pentagon and the Leckie Elementary school in Washington DC. I was also tasked with providing services to first responders who were charged with various responibilities immediately during the aftermath, and healing phase of the trauma throughout the city. For those who live in America, 9-11 was impossible to escape. The visual memory of that day lingered for years and continues to maintain an emotional grip on the lives of many people around the world.

The most significant thing to remember is that the process of grief and loss occurs in stages and it cannot be rushed. Allow it to heal in *Divine Time.*

The ability to share the grief that you may be experiencing is a major part of the healing process. When there has been a loss, bringing people together to talk about it is a major method for moving on successfully. In the Journey to finding Inner Peace, a group sharing, or the Power of the Circle experience is a highly effective tool for encouraging positive vibrations and healing. The following steps outline some ideas on how you can conduct a grief healing circle for sharing.

Grief Group Healing Circle Sharing Ideas:

1. Create a Safe Space for ensuring open communication and confidentiality.

2. State the Purpose ~ This allows the group to define why they are gathered.

3. There is healing in telling your own story in a creative way. Encourage poems, dance, songs, and personal stories. Have appropriate music to play.

4. Self-Reflection: Become a self-witness to how we are responding to grief and loss ~ asks the following questions:

    a. What is different now?

    b. Where do you feel grief in your body?

    c. What do you need to do right now?

    (Teach emotional release breathing exercises)

5. Allow each group member to form an intention of what they need to do now for healing.

6. Identify an emotional life support partner.

7. Gratitude Sharing Exercise: Encourage each participant to make a statement of gratitude.

8. What you put your attention on grows

and becomes permanent in your life group discussion.

    a. Continuously make positive statements about how you want your life to be.

    b. Practice visualization exercises to create a positive mental intention.

    c. Practice redirecting your thoughts from negative images.

9. Renewing Body, Mind, Spirit with the Power of Imagination...Visualization, Guided Imagery and Storytelling of safe and peaceful places.......calms the nervous system and releases fear and tension from the body.

Contact your local Mental Health agency and ask for help to cope with grief and loss or to assist you with creating a support group in your community. Remember, you are never alone God is always with you.

A Presence Is Watching Over You

THE HIGHER SELF....
A Reading Meditation Ritual

One of the deepest moments of despair in my life occurred when I found myself alone in my bedroom about 8 weeks after my husband decided to take a break from the marriage and move out of the house for a while. In the beginning, I spent my time doing every day activities and going on with life as usual, with the hopes in the back of my mind that this experience would be over quickly. There I was suddenly stricken by the most horrible sense of grief and despair that I have ever experienced in my life. The emotional pain was so unbearable that it brought back memories of a feeling that I thought I had left behind in the story line of my life years in the past. For some reason, the separation also evoked a code of silence. Knowing that there is power in the silence, I did everything in my power to honor it.

There I was, the master of my own emotions, crying hysterically and yelling at God, out loud, in anger and fear that my life had taken a turn that I could not control the outcome of. I tried everything that I knew, meditation, chanting, prayer, aromatherapy baths, psychotherapy, you name it I tried it. Nothing could stop the wrenching pain that I felt inside of my body. Not even chocolate had the soothing remedy of relief that I had become much too familiar with. A still deep inner voice began to speak with me that night, trying to convince me that the idea of death was the only way out of my despair. This feeling had also become much to familiar to me, and I knew that voice was not mine or the voice of God. Immediately I realized that I had to speak with my husband's Higher Self through my Higher Self. This approach to communication had not become a natural part of my personal communication style; however, I was willing to start it if I could find some inner peace with it. I was a new student of the teachings of the Ascended Masters, and I remembered a story that I read entitled, <u>Your Higher Self Will Help You, written by Elizabeth Clare Prophet in the little booklet entitled "Access the Power of Your Higher Self"</u>. The story acknowledges that the power of calling on the higher power of the creator to solve all of life's mysteries and challenges will result into inner peace and balance. The technique of using the higher intelligence to make life decisions can be accessed through prayer in the silence or out loud. For example, if you should misplace something in the house, you would call on the "Mighty I AM Presence, in the name of Christ, to help you, and before you know it, a vision of where to look shows up, and before you know it what you need is manifested. I am sure that we have all had those experiences before. That night I decided to pray out loud and call on the Mighty I AM Presence to help me. First I had to light a pink candle and treat my bedroom with rose oil for love by dropping the oil in the four corners of the room and at the door entrance. Next I went into a meditative thought by using the breath while lying down with my back on the bed. I instantly received the idea to visualize my husband's face and see him smiling and happy. Once I was able to vision this picture, I was directed by my Higher Self or the still small voice within to ask for permission to speak with my husband's higher self. I felt like I received permission and began to talk with his Higher Self. I told the presence how I was feeling and asked for the opportunity to speak face to face. The conversation went on for a long while, and at the end, I felt a body shift which seemed to relive me of a considerable amount of emotional pain and discomfort. It felt as though I had actually spoken with my husband and we had come to some mutual conclusions on how to deal with the situation directly. Shortly after that, one night after 11pm, my husband showed up at home and we had an enchanting evening with powerful expressions of love and a feeling of completion was achieved. We were whole again.

The Higher Self Reading Meditation

This is a very simple meditation that can be recorded onto a tape or Disc for you to listen to over and over again. The instructions for conducting this meditation are very simple. Read each line very slowly, as you take in the deeper meaning of each phrase. After every fourth line, stop and take three deep breaths. After the third breath, resume the reading and continue until you have completed the entire Reading Meditation. This is very powerful in a group setting, and can also be used for personal meditation. Simply read the meditation following the instructions while guiding the group as you read the meditation out loud.

THE HIGHER SELF MEDITATION

1. Unfailing Source of Love, guidance, inspiration
   and spiritual energy,
   The central Sun – a spiritual Sun concentrated
   light, energy, consciousness.
   The sun is light; it is God, father & mother,
   Oneness with all creation.

2. I am presence.
   Return to your Christ Self
   We are meant to become our higher Selves, the

real self

The higher self to direct daily – latent talent to be revealed.

3. The causal body – a storehouse of energy
   The Christ self- anointed …The body of the universal Christ.

4. Develop relationships with the; I am presence….
   The inner teacher, guardian/practice.
   As above….. so below.
   Meditation, contemplation, increases the flow of light\Flame in the heart.

5. Decrees
   I bless my Heart –Anoint my head with oil –and radiate healing energy from my hands.
   I Clean up, mutilate, disintegrate all first emotional and mental debris accumulated from child hood traumas to lover's quarrels, belittling comments from parents, teachers, siblings and friends.

6. The physical body is clogged with the residue from everything you have eaten, drunk, and inhaled. Pesticides to chemicals in foods, exotic herbs etc. Getting rid of this collective negative energy is the first step towards communion with the "I AM" presence and finding serenity.

7. Violet light surrounds my body

   My Heart ~ My Head ~ My Hands

   Dissolving memories of hatred; anger, anxiety and fear. I visualize with my mind's eye, this healing violet light surrounding my heart & pulsating with each beat of the light of God.

8. I see my mind being purified of all negative and limiting self-concepts such as ignorance and mental blocks. I can even see the cells of my brain being cleansed of pollution, drugs, chemicals, nicotine, toxic air, toxic thoughts …..etc.

   My hands are the instruments that I act with within the world.

9. I now direct the light energy from my hands outward into the universe, I see it surrounding my whole body, my entire life, my loving family, my responsible community, the peaceful world etc….

   See it dissolving the memories of everything you wish you hadn't done and everything you wish had not happened to you.

11. My higher Self is clear to me, I am whole and I am free.

   Do this healing ritual daily and find yourself moving with greater freedom, liberated from the burdens weighing your dreams down. Now you think more clearly and act more decisively in everything that you do in life.

And so it is.........Amen

Seek Insight, Intuition and Stillness

The Three D's — Death, Dying and Depression

I am reminded as I am writing this passage of my personal relationship with death, dying and depression, that it is an experience in my life, and I am always consciously aware of it. I close my eyes and see my veins encircled with liquid white light. Spinning around each blood vessel shining with sparkles like the Milky Way. I feel the liquid light penetrating into my cells and begin to pour all over me like being baptized in the chilly waters of the Jordan River. I feel myself slipping into the darkness where there is no pain......I know that there is a place to go that pain cannot survive. I know that there is a place that welcomes me into its bosom of protection. I see the clouds as they open up for me and I sense voices whispering to me, come, come, we are waiting for you, and I am aware of a total sense of peace and stillness deep within me, which is beckoning me into the clouds. My attention is drawn to my body as my mind and heart begins to communicate with one another. It is not time, release her, and release her into life so that she may live. I can remember pleading with my heart and mind, I cannot take the pain anymore, let me go to see just what it is all about. I can feel my body being lifted upward and my mind is floating with desire and despair. I am desperately trying to resist the mysterious calling into the opening of the bright white fluffy clouds. I do not know where the desire to die comes from or why it is calling me. I just know that when the clouds become bright and the sun's rays are beaming from the sky, it is as if they are calling me. I reach deep into my inner knowing and the power of the higher mind and release myself from the desire to die. I know that my reality is that I want the pain to die instead of me. And gently the urge disappears as if it never were a reality in my feeling world, and I keep on driving my car to my destination, and I am thinking that no one will know of my secret passageway into inner peace, the ultimate peace and serenity…death is not an option. I knew weeks ago that I was going to have to write about death, dying and depression after everyone that read this manuscript asked the question, what is your story? Why can you teach about this subject matter? "It appears that you have been through something", "You must reveal it now". Later I would receive phone calls from friends that know me well, telling me the same thing, encouraging me to self disclose.

However, they really didn't know the true details about my relationship with death, dying and depression, and I thought that no one would ever know. Depression has a tendency to call on death as a solution to the pain. What I am very clear about is this; suicide is not the answer to true inner peace. It is only a tricky illusion that comes in an instant, just at the right time to take your life from you prematurely. I know that if you are challenged with clinical depression, the desire to "end it all" is familiar to you. I have been encouraged to talk about my personal experience for several reasons. Reason number one; it is time to release my pain and sadness into the world and find healing for myself. Reason number two; is so that I may serve as a source of inspiration for others who no longer believe that they can find themselves again because of depression. I am here to tell you and the world that you have never been lost, depression is the passageway into life transformation, and I know that I have been transformed to reprogram my beliefs about what depression represents in my life. We are always becoming greater than what and who we are. As I think back on my life journey, I realize that anxiety played a huge role in my life and resulted into eczema, shortness of breath and chronic fear as young child. Even though I was very outgoing, energetic and scholarly, anxiety and depression found its way into life. I was seventeen years old and in college when I first realized that I needed some help to relive the tension in my body. The tension and anxiety became so overpowering that it was distracting and eventually debilitating. Depression can stand in the way of inner peace and serenity, therefore, I have decided to talk about the specifics of depression in an effort to offer the information required to deal with it, release it and transform it into inner peace. The first step is to determine if depression plays a role in your life and if so, at what level is it present. All human life at some point will experience good times and bad times, joy and sadness. However, if the feelings of sadness and melancholy last for more than a few weeks at a time, or you find yourself having difficulty in your day to day life management, you may be challenged with what I consider to be a very serious medical condition, Clinical Depression. Secondly, Major Depressive Disorder (depression) is not just a temporary mood, and it's not a sign of personal weakness. Depression is a serious medical condition with a variety of symptoms. Emotional symptoms can include sadness, loss of interest in things you once enjoyed, feelings of guilt or worthlessness, restlessness, and trouble concentrating or making decisions. Physical symptoms can include fatigue, vague aches and pains, migraine headaches, and changes in weight or sleep patterns. For some, depression can include thoughts of death or suicide. During these times of Hope and Change, we must all become more sensitively aware of the emotional symptoms of stress, dis-stress, anxiety and fear. Many people suffer in silence while depression slowly eats away at their quality of life. Some are ashamed or afraid to seek help; others try to downplay the severity of their symptoms. It's important to remember that depression isn't something that's "all in your head." People with a family history of depression may be more likely to get the disease, but anyone can become depressed. Sometimes the triggers are external—for example, relationship troubles or financial problems. At other times the disease may begin with physical illness or hormonal shifts. Depression also may occur without any identifiable trigger at all.

Depression is common, affecting about 121 million people worldwide. More than 32 million people in the United States will experience a major depressive episode in their lifetime. This happens regardless of gender, race, ethnicity, or income. Depression can affect friends and family as well. Unfortunately, many people with depression avoid seeking treatment because they worry what others will think of them. They don't realize how widespread this medical condition is:

- Depression is among the leading causes of disability worldwide

- Women are nearly twice as likely as men to experience depression

- People with a family history of depression may be more likely to develop the disease

- People with chronic or debilitating medical conditions may also be susceptible to the disease

- A major life change, even a joyous one like becoming a new parent, increases the risk of developing depression

- The fact is depression affects plenty of people who don't have any obvious risk factors

- If you are concerned about some of your symptoms, here are a few important first steps on the journey into healing:

Learn more about depression

The term depression refers to a lasting sad mood and/ or a loss of interest or pleasure in the things you enjoy doing in life. Depression is a serious medical condition and should be treated by a mental health professional. Depression involves the body, mood, and thoughts. It affects eating habits, sleeping habits and relationships with others. A depressive disorder is not the same as an occasional blue mood. It is not a sign of personal weakness or a condition that can be willed or wished away. People challenged with depression cannot just, "pull themselves or get themselves together", like many people often say. Without the proper treatment, symptoms could last for weeks, months and even years. Learn more about how depression affects the emotions and the body, and read about the various treatments available before speaking with a healthcare professional. You can also make a list of questions to ask during your visit about your symptoms or concerns related to the changes in your life.

Most importantly.........do something, anything about it. Your life depends on it. If thoughts of suicide are prevalent in your life, contact your local suicide prevention agency by calling 411 or 911 if you feel that your impulses and/or thoughts are out of control.

As a Holistic Psychotherapist, I like to examine depression from an integrative health perspective, which considers the mind, body and spirit equally in diagnosing its cause and recommending treatment modalities. Treatment of this nature is focused on using the *Soul Language* to determine treatment intervention. The Mind-Body-Spirit or what I like to call the Tri- Consciousness of human existence, is the primary approach to holistic psychotherapy. The mind is not synonymous with the brain, the mind uses the brain and nervous system to function, thus creating the Mind/Body connection. As mentioned in earlier chapters, the spirit interfaces with the body through the functioning of the endocrine glandular system. When there is dysfunction in any one of the states of Tri Consciousness (Mind/Body/Spirit), there is a distortion of the wholeness of the self. Metaphysical study reveals that the concept of a depressed state, speaks literally to what is occurring in the nerve impulses of the human anatomy. Dysfunction of the glandular system, such as adrenal, pineal, thyroid and pancreas are commonly contributing to depressed states of awareness. This state of "beingness" can sometimes be associated with toxins in the system from poor elimination, accumulated poisons and lack of cellular movement and regeneration. There is also a psychosomatic aspect to depressed states of consciousness and awareness due to negative thought forms and attitudes that can cause degeneration in the nerve impulses of the central nervous system. Eventually, that pathological thought system becomes a self-destructive behavioral pattern, leading to depression and destructive emotional and mental congestion. Holistic Treatment for depression is a very powerful and transforming experience. An integrative treatment approach is highly recommended for depression on all levels, combined with talk therapy or psychotherapy interventions. Suggestions for integrating holistic treatment with contemporary mental health modalities are listed below;

1. The first approach to relieving the body of toxic waste is to improve the process of **bowel elimination**. When the nerve impulses in the body become highly toxic, the emotional feeling of being depressed occurs. Therefore, it is a logical approach to relieve the body of the toxins which create the negative effects of the nervous system. This can be done by drinking plenty of water, deep muscle massage therapy, steam baths, colonics and skin brushing.

2. **Prayer and meditation** addresses the spiritual side of treatment for the Tri-Consciousness emotional revival. We now know that consciousness can penetrate bio-photons in the body, therefore the power of thought forms can create significant transformation within the human anatomy.

3. **Synergy movement fitness** exercise is a significant attribute to creating relaxation and stress release. For better results, conduct the exercise in fresh air out of doors and remember to take long deep breaths with rhythmic movement.

4. **Visualization and Guided Imagery** therapies are powerful treatment modalities for counteracting the effects of depressed moods. The power of the mind is an awesome process to witness. The scientific

truth of brain functioning demonstrates why visualization and guided imagery is such an effective method for healing. The brain has the capacity of translating a mental image into physiological reality. In other words, the brain does not know the difference between reality and visual imagery. If this is the case, then we can create a new reality by simply visualizing it, stimulating a sensory response within the body. Visualization and Guided Imagery Therapy allows one to actually see and feel healing occurring during healing sessions.

If you are determined to manifest inner peace and you feel that you just cannot do anything about the depression... on your own........remember to use the silence, seek stillness, intuition .....and insight....

Hold on... Trust That Healing is on the Way.

CHAPTER FIVE

Relaxation and Meditation Healing Rituals

Aromatherapy Spiritual Bath Rituals

The Healing Chamber

I'm in this inner healing chamber, awaiting the high priests for the ritual of insight, intuition, and stillness. Colon cleaning and the laying on of hands in the healing Crystal Chamber deep inside of mother earth.

It fit right into my fire and water healing meditation.

The ritual began with the preparation of the Aromatherapy, the fire earn and the spiritual bath #1.

Given to me by a Native American Shaman named Baba Ade.

He came from New York to facilitate the healing for me.

The fire meditation revealed an intense force of energy directed towards my hands.

The fire spoke encouraging me to focus on the universal healing music over and over again.

The affirmation came, trust....... the universe will provide.

Focus your attention on these directions…ase'

The bath journey began

The bath was taken in the green energy for protection and strength.

The inner journey continued from last night.

There I was on top of a huge crystal that was flat on the top and about 8 feet in diameter.

On the sides of the flat surface was a straight drop that appeared to be endless, like a bottomless pit.

The angels appeared again and one of them started to take the shape of my great grandmother's face and then it faded.

Another felt like my grandmother.

The feeling of the presence remained and they became light bodies.

These beings began to lay hands on me and a great sense of comfort overwhelmed me.

Deep love was felt and expressed and transmitted.

It seemed as if they were offering everything that I needed.

They bathed me with oceans of light, and the light became another crystal tunnel.

I began to travel through the tunnel into pure darkness.

The voice came and encouraged me not to be afraid.

At this point my Christian education started to say

You could be in danger

You are going downward but quickly I changed the thought

And heard the voice say…release the fear…god is with you.

Shortly after the crystal tunnel began to swirl and swirl into a spiral and I realized that I was in my own colon.

The voice said you must first clean out the colon of all foreign matter and

Suddenly I was back on the flat surface of the crystal.

A quartz crystal appeared and became a pendulum.

The pendulum swung directly over my third eye, back and forth, and back and forth.

As this was going on…. The light beings returned and began to rattle all around my body with Native American instruments, especially in areas needing the most healing.

The voice spoke.

Seek insight, intuition and stillness.

While I was in the crystal healing chamber, a huge quartz crystal with a double point rolled from the top of my head to my feet, around my body to the other side and made a complete circle around me.

This was approximately three to four feet above my head.

I was aware of an electromagnetic field that surrounded the space around me.

It felt like a protective shield.

*The water is healing to the soul
and soothing to the mind*

Protect Yourself

Spiritual Bath Ritual Regeneration Recipes

The Spiritual Bath Regeneration Process is rebuilding healthy cells in the body. Energizing dis-easesd cells with the healing bath is an ancient practice of the masters. This is the way to keep our bodies vigorous, energized and whole. Practice vigorous dry brush massage starting at your feet and working upwards towards the heart before each bath ritual.

Bath # 1- External Cleansing

On the Path to Healthy Cells.

Regeneration is rebuilding and energizing healthy cells in the body. This is the secret of the ancient Kemitic Masters, the way to keeping our bodies vigorous and healthy.

4 drops of Eucalyptus oil

7-10 pounds of Epsom salt (Urgent Health Note: salt should not be used if you have high blood pressure, use natural herbs, i.e. lavender buds, eucalyptus leaves, essential oils etc.) If you use the natural herbs, you must crush the herbs and place them in a poultice bag before putting them into the bath water.

Take this bath 3-4 times a week for external cleansing.

Soak the body for 20 minutes in hot bath water. While in

the bath, massage the body vigorously in upward motions towards the heart. Relax for the last five minutes of the bath. Allow the water to drain while still in the tub. After all of the water has drained take a cool to warm shower and pat dry the body.

Bath # 2- Spiritual Cleansing

To take this journey, a spiritual cleansing bath is recommended. It offers sacred moments for the removal of adverse energy in your auric field. You might ask "what do you mean by this"? Most of us have experienced periodic spiritual upsets resulting from tension in relationships, problems in life, on the job, arguments with family members, finances, you know what I mean. Occurrences such as these can literally cause you to feel tension all around you. Some very sensitive people can even notice the energy after a stressful event, argument or emotional upset. The atmosphere actually changes and feels unsettling. A spiritual bath can help to resolve the negativity of "**bad vibes**". It is necessary that you cleanse the bathroom that you are taking your journey in. As time goes on, you should begin to practice spiritual cleansing of your entire home frequently as well. The results of the spiritual bath will be peaceful, and balancing. It also offers a feeling of being well grounded.

In a hot to warm bathtub of water:

Mix 4 tablespoons of sea salt

½ box of baking soda

Slowly lower yourself into the tub and rest your back on a tub pillow. Sit for 15-20 minutes while sponging your skin with the treated water. During this time, pray for healing and releasing negative thoughts, feelings, memories etc. When you have completed your bath, step very carefully out of the tub *after* you have pulled the plug to the drain. ***Do not pull the plug after you have gotten out* of the tub**. If you forget, use a coat hanger or something that will open the drain without you placing your hands back into the water. You will feel the difference immediately!

Bath #3- Ocean Rinse

Fill two one gallon plastic jugs with ocean water. Place 15 drops of lavender essential oil in both jugs and shake them for about 20 seconds, one jug at a time. Pour the ocean water over your entire body in an outdoor shower, secured back patio or bathtub. It is a great experience if you have an outdoor shower to try this rinse. It is also a natural high to pour the aroma sea water on your body while standing on the beach with your feet in the water. Allow the sun to dry the skin while you practice meditation after the rinse in the nude. If it is not possible to meditate nude, in privacy outside, go inside and complete a meditation after the rinse.

Bath #4 -Sand Bath

Mother Earth offers the mind, body and spirit the opportunity for healing and cleansing poisons from the system. Sand baths can purify the skin, bring you closer to God and increase blood circulation for relaxation. Prior to taking a sand bath, drink 24 ounces of spring water with lemon juice. Have a 16-18 ounce glass of spring water ready for after the sand bath.

Locate a spot to dig a body hole for you to get into on the beach.

You will need assistance from someone to pack the sand onto your body from neck to toe.

Be sure that you are comfortable in the body hole and then relax for up to 20 minutes.

Have your sand bath partner close by observing you as you allow the sun's rays to recharge your spirit and energize your body by stimulating the sand. Be sure to have sun protection in the case of hot sun rays.

After 20 minutes, begin to dig the sand out from around your body starting at the feet. Slowly remove yourself from the sand. Once you have been completely removed from the body hole, vigorously wipe your skin clean of the sand with a white terry cloth towel.

Drink your 8 ounces of spring water, and then relax for the rest of the day.

Avoid any rigorous activity for at least 8 hours.

Bath #5- Steam Bath

Place 15 drops of eucalyptus oil on the floor of a steam room or hot shower. Be sure to close the door and place the oil on the floor while the steam is being dispersed. Be careful not to get the oil in your eyes or slip on the oil. Sit or stand in the steam room and inhale deeply and slowly. This is a very refreshing bath experience, good for relieving mental and lung congestion. This steam ritual is a wonderful energizer for the day. For this ritual you can use any essential oil of your choice.

Bath #6- Deep Pore Cleansing

Soaking in warm water enables the body to release toxins through the skin, the largest organ in the body. Smudging the bathroom with white sage or lemongrass will help create a sacred space and pure experience.

Pour a combination of 10-12 pounds of Epsom salt and/ or dead sea salt into a hot bath of running water.

Place 10 drops of eucalyptus oil into the running water.

Slowly enter the bath water and sit without covering your heart with the water. Caution: (this could increase your heart rate rapidly, so be mindful not to cover your heart with the bath water)

Optional: You can place 3 drops of peppermint oil in Afrikan shae butter or sunflower oil and rub it onto your chest.

Scrub your body with a loofah sponge or natural hair brush in an upward motion towards your heart.

Follow with a brisk cool shower.

Dry your body well and anoint it with body oil or cream.

Bath #7- Foot Baths

Cold Water foot baths will stimulate circulation and relieve heavy tired feet. Do not use cold water if your feet are already cold. Place 2 drops of peppermint oil in the cold water and soak your feet for as long as you can take it. Remove your feet and rub them with a foot warming cream. Cover your feet with white socks and rest them for at least one hour on a stack of pillows. Read your favorite book or look at a real good movie, or take a nap. Just do not move for a while.

Hot Water foot baths help to relax the whole body, mind and spirit. Place Aloe Vera bubbles, sea salt, baking soda and 10 drops of wintergreen essential oil in a vibration foot bath tub. Soak your feet for 15-20 minutes with vibration and pat dry. Cover your feet with white socks and rest them on a stack of pillows.

Bath # 8- Facial Steam Bath

This bath is effective for cleansing facial skin and releasing toxins in the pores. Pour 5 quarts of water into a cooking pot. Bring the water to a boil over the stove and turn off the fire. Place 3 drops of honeysuckle oil in the water. Cover the cooking pot and your head with a white towel while placing your face in the steam. Be careful not to get too close to the hot steam. Continue this ritual until you feel complete, and then, pat dry your skin and put a moisturizer on your facial skin. Ahhhhhhh

Bath #9- Holy Honey Bath

Place 10-15 drops of grapefruit essential oil into running bath water.

Pour one cup of natural raw honey into running bath water. Be sure that the water is hot enough to melt the honey.

Pour one to two cups of honey into a glass dish and place it on the side of the bathtub near your head.

Add 1-15 drops of your favorite bubble bath into the water and allow it to lather...

Slowly (be careful not to step into water that is too hot) enter the bath water and rest your head on the bath pillow and relax for a while..

Begin to massage your skin with the raw honey that is in the glass dish, and enjoy the smooth longs strokes of your hands on your skin, while you are basking in the sweetness of the honey onto your skin.

Rinse with warm shower water and pat dry.

Ooooooooo.....Ahhhhhhhhhhhhh

Bath #10- Sea Salt Bath DO NOT TAKE ANY SALT BATHS IF YOU HAVE HIGH BLOOD PRESSURE. CONSULT YOUR PHYSICAN FIRST. USE ESSENTIAL OILS AND DRY HERBAL LEAVES ONLY FOR YOUR BATH RITUALS. (make a poultice bag for all herbal leaf baths)

Sea Salt added to bathwater helps remove toxic substances from your body. It cleanses the whole system. Minerals in sea salt help strengthen the immune system and activate the Auric Field.

Relaxing Sea Salt Bath: Place 20 Drops of lavender and jasmine essential oils into 2 cups of sea salt and blend for 3 minutes.

Detoxifying Bath: Place 5 drops of lemon, 6 drops of juniper berry & 10 drops of eucalyptus essential oils directly into bath water.

Inner Peace Bath: Pour two cups of your favorite non toxic bubble bath into a glass bowl. Drop 15- 20 drops of lavender essential oil into the bowl. Slowly stir the mixture until a throfty substance appears and then pour the mixture into running hot water for the bath.

Energy Bath: Pour two cups of your favorite non toxic bubble bath into a glass bowl. Drop 15- 20 drops of peppermint and 10 drops of lemongrass essential oils into the bowl. Slowly stir the mixture until a throfty substance appears and then pour the mixture into running hot water for the bath.

Emotional Release Bath: Pour two cups of your favorite non toxic bubble bath and baking soda into a glass bowl. Drop 15- 20 drops of blue chamomile and jasmine essential oils into the bowl. Slowly stir the mixture until a throfty substance appears and then pour the mixture into running hot water for the bath.

Muscle Tension Bath : : Pour two cups of your favorite

non toxic bubble bath and 1 pound of Epsom salt into a glass bowl. Drop 15- 20 drops of eucalyptus and 1-=12 drops of wintergreen essential oils into the bowl. Slowly stir the mixture until a throfty substance appears and then pour the mixture into running hot water for the bath.

Instructions for blending the salt with the essential oils:

1. Pour four cups of sea salt into a mixing bowl.

2. With a wooden mallet or large wooden spoon, blend the oil into the salt.

3. Be sure to blend the oil into the salt well, until you notice a powered like substance.

Bath #11 Alkaline Bath

Run a tub of warm water. Heat will increase your blood flow, so keep the water a little cool. Add one cup of sea salt and one cup of bicarbonate of soda to the tub. This is a highly alkaline mixture and I recommend using it only once or twice a month. It is very helpful with relieving muscle pain, cramps and irritable anxiety. Soak for at least 20 minutes. This will help you to feel very relaxed and sleepy. You will wake up feeling refreshed and energized.

The Bath Interlude

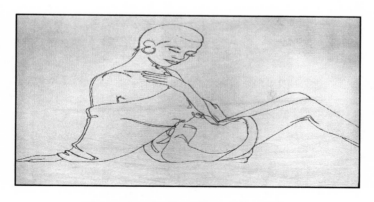

Illustration: by Ron "Iceman" Wallace

Ingredients for the Bath

1. Aromatherapy bath salts. (four cups)

2. Bath tub head rest.

3. Candles (as many as you desire, lots of candles) remember to secure your candles well inside of a glass container!!!

4. Peppermint natural liquid soap.

5. Loofa sponge.

6. Natural bath foam or bubbles (lots of bubbles) warning!!! Be careful not to use too much if using a Jacuzzi bathtub....Just a dab will do ya.

7. Extra large white terry cloth bath towel.

8. Comfortable attire for after bath.

9. One bottle of bubbling apple cider.

10. One champagne fluke.

11. Piano music playing in the back drop of the Bath Ritual.

Instructions:

Run bath water hot as you can stand. Pour bath salts into running water followed by bath foam. Put the head rest in a comfortable position and light the candles. Be sure that you will not be disturbed by anything once you are in the divine bath essence. **PRIVACY IS ABSOLUTELY NECESSARY!!!!!!!!!!!!**

ALERT!!!!!! DO NOT FALL ASLEEP!!!

Take a deep breath and exhale slowly to the count of 10 and then relax. Do this exercise several times until you become completely relaxed. Try not to concentrate on any one thought. Just let the thoughts flow…. As you become aware of the gentle bubbles and the soothing salt aromatic water embracing your body, enjoy your bubbling cider and thoughts of your dreams and deepest heart desires, eventually not concentrating on any one thought. After soaking for at least 20 minutes, put some peppermint soap on the loofa mitt and begin to massage the skin. Put more pressure on your elbows, knees and feet. Stand up and rinse yourself with the sponge until all of the bubbles are rinsed from your body.

Step out of the tub carefully and pat yourself dry. Massage some type of oil or body cream into the skin from head to toe. Put on your comfortable night lounging clothing.

Now, lay back and enjoy the sensations of total relaxation.

Emotional Healing

Our emotions are stored deep within the human body at a cellular level. It is my belief that we even store trauma and memories in the cells of the body. The emotions tend to tell the story of the past, future and present moment by manifesting facial expression, body posture and even skin texture and color. Emotions carry a very strong physical energy and can cause exhaustion and even chronic fatigue, or it can manifest positive energy, personal power and successful outcomes in life. Often times our emotions can determine the outcomes of life circumstances and even resolve deep wounds that cannot be seen by the human eye. With correct intention, specific meditative thought forms and effective visualization, emotional healing can be achieved.

The process of emotional healing involves retraining the brain to accept new thoughts for enhanced living. The following Emotional Grounding Meditative Thoughts are healing rituals for calming the heart and mind. As you contemplate each meditative thought, create a mental image of integrating each word with your left and right brain, by imagining the words flowing through each cell in the brain. It helps to enhance the experience by allowing your eyes to follow the thoughts flowing through the brain, by rolling your eyes from left to right, with your eyes closed. Starts with the thought form number one….. infinite love….and continue focusing on that thought until you are ready to move to the next thought form. It is not necessary to complete every thought in one session. You can select a few of the thoughts or just concentrate on one, the choice is yours. Remember to take deep breaths and allow your shoulders to droop down, down, down, during the Emotional Grounding Meditation Ritual.

The Greatest Healer is Love

Emotional Grounding Meditative Thoughts

1. Infinite love

2. Infinite wisdom

3. Harmony

4. Healing

5. Life

6. Light

7. Success

8. Possibility

9. Health

10. Hope

11. Energy

12. Courage

13. Strength

14. Infinite peace

Emotional Release Body Rituals

Create an Emotional Charge Deep Within You

Emotional Grounding Rituals for Mental Clarity

1. Experience any fear that most concerns you at this time. Experience this fear as sound. Visualize it as white light located above the crown of your head.

2. Surrender or release the sound of your fear by attaching the constant "M" to the end of it. Like AAHM, RAHM OR HEEM Sense the harmonic sound of your essence.

Lam   (Red)...............Vam   (Orange)................
Ram (Yellow)..............Yam (Green).............Ham
(Blue) ....Aum (Indigo)..................Ommmm
(Violet)..............

3. Empower this harmony by inhaling deeply and pronouncing the sound you created in step 2, drawing it over the course of your entire exhalation. Repeat for six times.

4. Nurture the harmony by staying with it as

you feel a deep sense of awareness of your inner harmony. As you chant, feel the future coming into harmony with your sense of trust.

5. Create an emotional charge with the sound deep within you.

6. Embody the energy of trust by visualizing your entire physical body being composed of billions of cells. Visualize the cells as being composed of trillions of atoms. Visualize the atoms moving as well as the vast amount of space within and between them.

7. While playing your singing crystal bowl, meditation bell, energy chime or healing instrument, chant your essence sound.

8. Close the ritual with a praise prayer of your choice.

Sounding Away Pain

Emotional Release Toning Ritual

Toning can stabilize the emotions and relax the body

I'M NOT EXACTLY SURE WHEN IT ALL BEGAN. I REMEMBER THE FIRST TIME THAT I EXPERIENCED THE HEALING POWERS OF

SOUND & TONING. It was approximately 10 o'clock PM when my water broke and I realized that I was on my way to becoming a mother for the first time. My mind was racing and my heart beating fast and I knew this was it, no stopping it now, my son was on his way to his new life on earth and all that I could think about was the pain.

I had just returned home from a five-day in-patient stay at the Booth Memorial Hospital in Cleveland, Ohio, after being diagnosed with Braxton Hicks, "false labor pains." My pregnancy was very difficult and I found myself in my doctor's office almost three to four times a week. It seemed as thought I was always challenged with some type of illness or intense pain that had no apparent diagnosis.

No sooner than I returned home, my water broke and I found myself right back at the same hospital in the same bed, with same nurses that I had the week before. During my pregnancy, I learned the Lamaze method and felt pretty prepared for what was to come. However, the now x-husband, failed to see the importance of learning the Lamaze method with me, so there I was, preparing myself for the unknown with a husband who had only been nominally involved in the nine month pregnancy and who, it appeared, would not be part of the actual birth experience. And I said nothing.

I realize now that my acceptance of negative pain was

one of the primary sources of my habit of holding onto emotional trauma, accepting negative people, negative behaviors and painful experiences into my life. I would never speak up for myself and tell how I truly felt, for fear of rejection. At that time the now X-husband was in the beginning stages of his alcohol and cocaine addiction, and I was unaware of it. Not realizing that he could not be present with me, I decided to internalize the emotional pain and blame myself and told myself that I had to be strong.

I was very brave, and had decided to have a natural birth, so I stuck with the plan in spite of my surroundings. The contractions were fairly easy until "the transition". Then the pain became more and more intense. I asked "the now x- husband" to massage my lower back and stand with me, hold my hand or something, anything, to help me deal with the pain. All he could do was start yelling and telling me to "be strong "and "stop crying." When I could not do the latter, he said, "You are stupid," and left the room.

I was alone in the birthing room with my familiar companion, emotional pain, now compounded by the physical challenges of child birth.

I bore the pain as well as I could. Then, somewhere between the moments of precious breath, tears of sadness and the wrenching spiral motions of the contractions, I found myself beginning a low grade hum which eventually became long and deep descending sounds in rhythmic timing with each contraction. Because I found a major relief with this, I noticed that I was intentionally creating the sounds to relieve the tension and pain. Shortly after establishing a long and rhythmic flow of this pattern, my doctors informed me that I was dilating at increased speed and that the birth would be sooner than expected. Everything seemed to speed up and in the midst of all of the drama the now X-husband came yelling that my OB/GYN had been killed in an automobile accident. I would have to be attended by a doctor that I didn't even know.

A bit desperate, I focused on the **tones** that were coming to me, resonating throughout my entire body and my mind. I was focused on creating a calm awareness and connecting with the great challenge that my son was experiencing in his long awaited entrance into the world. Years later, I learned that I was engaged in a technique called **Toning**, which synchronizes and balances brainwaves and reduces stress, pain and negative emotions. The toning must have served as an internal vibrational massage of the birthing canal, allowing my cervix to contract much faster than usual. I dilated so fast, that the doctors had no time to prepare my body for the birth. My son came into this world with a fast sliver of rhythmic movement through the birth canal on the **waves of sound.**

My inner **keynotes** of life force energy brought life into this world.

Now, the use of toning didn't just pop into my mind, I had already been a student and practitioner of metaphysics and spiritual enlightenment for at least 5 years prior to this experience, so I was already aware of alternative methods of healing and had begun to use some of the concepts in my work as a psychotherapist. However, I had never used toning specifically for healing. This was a new experience that would stay deeply embedded in my mind for some time before I realized its true value. Sound became a regular passageway for my personal healing, and would eventually become the medium that **saved my emotional life.** Being more sensitively aware of sound and the impact that it had on my son's birth, I had universal permission to open my mind to look beyond the normal and accept a new way of being.

Solar Plexus Meditation Ritual

The emotional body is specifically located in the Sacral Chakra, located between the navel and genitalia. The emotional body is also located in the solar plexus, just above the navel and below the chest cavity. Chronic emotional stress is caused by unresolved (and usually unrecognized) negative emotional issues. Often the results of emotional reactions to stressful events in childhood or even other lifetimes, become stored and forgotten like old toys or memories from the past. Although forgotten, along with the events that caused them, they continually drain energy from the body system. Negative emotional issues are stored in the emotional body and cells as energetic thought-forms accompanied by a strong emotional frequency. These stored emotional issues cause us to automatically overreact to similar events in present time, further reinforcing the stress. The intensity of the emotional reaction to a current event may be out of all proportion to the significance of the event itself. This is possible evidence that stress stores in our cells as emotional memory.

We often work hard to clear our minds of negative beliefs and thought patterns. We forge ahead on our spiritual path; and support our physical bodies through healthy lifestyle choices. In spite of diligently doing our homework, memorable fears and old resentments keep surfacing to remind us that we still feel powerless, and unlovable. Until we are able to recognize the intensity of the frequency, it has a tendency to repeat itself over and over again. In order to completely and permanently release a negative emotional issue, it is not essential to remember when it originated. Every similar event in present time that triggers the same emotional frequency is energetically connected to that original event. It is the emotional frequency that holds the pattern in storage until it is consciously activated and released. Once a specific issue has been identified, the associated emotional frequency is activated by bringing it to the conscious level within the physical body. Once the emotional charge is released from the body, it can no longer affect our behavior even though we may continue to remember the event(s) that caused it. This ritual is designed to assist you with the releasing of old emotional frequency patterns. Begin this ritual by conducting a sacral, solar plexus Meditation Ritual in the Key of D and E.

PAY CLOSE ATTENTION TO WHAT YOU SEE & FEEL DURING THIS RITUAL.

Allow your mind to go on a deep discovery within yourself

The Solar Plexus chakra is directly connected to the pancreas. The pancreas controls the liver, digestive system, stomach, spleen, gall bladder, autonomic nervous system, lower back muscles. The emotional responsibility of the Solar Plexus is the creation of personal power, social identity, influence, authority, and self control.

The Sacral Chakra is directly connected to the reproductive organs. The reproductive organs control the pelvic area, sexual organs, potency, fluid functions, kidneys and bladder. The emotional responsibility of the sacral chakra is the function of prima feelings, sexuality, desire, sensuality, procreation, pleasure, and personal creativity.

Resent research conducted by UCLA has concluded that each cell in the body has a distinctive sound wave pattern. Cancerous cells have specific tonal quality that is dramatically different than healthy cells. I conclude that by creating specific sound wave frequencies within and without the body, the cells can be nurtured to balance and regenerate themselves. This is the function & practice of Synergistic Healing.

Emotional Release Toning Ritual

The First Instruction for conducting this Meditation Ritual directs you to finding the key of D & E on your keyboard or Master Key Pitch instrument made by WM. KRATT CO USA. If you are not a musician or familiar with the notes on the keyboard, it is suggested that once you locate the notes on the keyboard, mark them for future reference with easily removable tape. A great book to purchase to guide you is entitled, "Start Reading Music", by Amy Appleby. The book has pictures of the notes and keyboard to make it easy to label your keyboard.

Begin this Toning Ritual with three deep cleansing breaths. Take a deep breath through the nose and exhale through the mouth. Notice any tension in your shoulders, lower back and release it. Continue to take the cleansing breaths and slowly begin to Tone the vowel sounds; inhale, exhale A; inhale, exhale E; inhale, exhale I; inhale, exhale O; inhale, exhale U, in the key of D and E. You can create your own toning combinations. Remember to inhale first, taking a long and deep breath, filling your lungs with air. Then exhale slowly the tone of the key note, expelling all of the air in your diaphragm. Remember to use the instructions given on the correct breathing technique.

No More Worries

THERE WAS A POINT IN MY LIFE WHEN I BEGAN TO SELF MEDICATE WITH PRESCRIPTION DRUGS. Pain had become a major theme for me, and it consumed my very being. The pain was not only physical; it was also emotional and psychological. At the time I did not know it, but I was suffering from depression and it came to me in expressions of pain. I had pain in my marital relationship, my physical body, my family relationships, work experiences, with creativity, finances etc. However, I quickly realized self medication was leading to a dependency on prescription drugs that were very harmful and I was well aware of the destructive nature of this practice. It was the pain that drew me closer to nature and led me on this great quest for knowledge about the origin of things as a way of healing. I reached a point in my early twenties when I felt that the pain was too much to bear as my nights became nightmares and my days became long moments of contemplated death. In my heart I knew that life was much more than constant pain and suffering, and my **real self** did not want to die. As a therapist, I knew that depression brought suffering and pain and this understanding served as a reality check for me. However, it did not stop the pain and suffering. All I wanted was to get out of it, and death kept showing up in my mind. There were very few people that I could talk to about this. My family did not seem to understand what I was experiencing. I think that they may have formed some opinions about my behavior and did not see it as a need for help, compassion and understanding. After all, I was the therapist, and it was my job to so call "heal others". Therefore, much of my suffering was in the silence. Much later, on my journey to freedom, I realized that silence was a place that I could go for ideas on what to do, however, to keep silent about one's pain can be very dangerous.

One night I was in so much pain, that I began to try and figure out how I could really kill myself. In that instance, I remembered a tape that my aunt Mattie Robinson had given me years before, entitled "Meditation" by Brother AH. Now, seven years prior in 1975, I had become a student of meditation. At that time I paid a fee and my teacher/ mentor, Paulette Bell, taught me a method called **Transcendental Meditation**. My grandmother paid for the class because she must have known that depression was a theme in my life, or maybe she just knew that I was suffering with emotional pain and wanted to help me.

As I was contemplating taking my own life to be free of pain, I decided to play the tape because I could remember the **peace** that meditation brought to me. As soon as the music began to play, I cried, and my entire being became consumed with the **sounds of awareness...**I felt the music penetrating my cells; a vibration deep within me seemed to be releasing the pain from my body.

I wondered what was happening to me with this music that I had never heard or felt before. The sounds seemed to give me life, hope and visions; I felt a sense of purpose, relief and serenity. Sounds such as these, healing, peaceful, sounds became my **music medicine** in times of my sadness and despair.

The **music medicine** became a refuge for my survival and was the beginning of a new way of life, understanding and practice. For years, I wondered why music had such a major impact on my mind, body and spirit. Why did my consciousness appear to become more enlightened and my life reach deeper spiritual experiences when the vibrations of sound were present? I felt more at peace, more whole, more serene with healing music as my guide.

This newly found state of serenity and confidence gave me the strength to leave an extremely verbally violent and emotionally abusive relationship with the X husband, and it gave me a new beginning to life. Meditation had offered me safe passage and moments of hope and inner peace that I thought had been lost forever.

During this time of my life journey, there was one thing that I realized, although silence about pain can be harmful, the silence, the true inner silence, is one of our greatest gifts. I learned that the silence is the place that toning & meditation eventually takes us to. Later in life I learned that silence is also a form of sound healing. I could find the still small voice within, in the silence. Silence helped me to quiet the mental chatter that was distracting my attention from the voice of God. It was in the silence that I learned the answers to all of my heart's deepest desires and needs. The silence that rests within the music of healing, the no tone, is where the healing is found. Just like any other medicine, toning & meditation helps the body to accomplish its own healing.

Healing Affirmations

I knew very early in my life that positive affirmations could make life a more pleasant experience than being obsessed with fear and doubt. The power of obtaining an affirmative mind set can change your life and even outcomes and circumstances of life. Repetitive affirmations are another process of retraining the brain to accept new concepts, ideas and intentions. While reciting affirmations, you are creating a declaration of commitment claiming a thing to be true. The brain responds physiologically to what messages the mind sends. Therefore, by creating affirmative thoughts, the brain will send the message to the central nervous system to accept the affirmation and respond. Affirmations rewire the brain and nervous system to accept positive attraction.

The Healing Affirmation Ritual

Repeat the following affirmations with vigor and excitement. Commit this ritual to memory to enhance its power effect.

- **I accept myself completely just as I am**

- **I am full of radiant light energy full of vigor and stamina**
- **My personal power is growing stronger every day**
- **I feel my creativity streaming through my body, soul & mind**
- **My creativity/sexual energy has power to create and transform**
- **I open myself to others naturally**
- **I am pure health, I am pure wellness & I am whole**

The Voice Said

The fire blazed high as ten feet, then suddenly the voice said:

"This is how I love you"

The flame was full, intense, and vibrant;

It appeared to keep on coming more and more.

As the voice directed my thoughts, I realized that

I want to love God the same way that God loves me,

fully with intensity and fire energy.

And then the voice said

"Have patience with life"

Just relax and allow things to manifest, as you love me intensely and fully.

The word patience and the voice said

Look deeply for the meaning of things in life

Always contemplate deeper into things

The fire inspired the voice to say

Follow your hearts desires and

Love faith

Moving Forward

Agnihotra Fire Purification Meditation Ritual

Agnihotra is an ancient scientific practice at sunrise and sunset to bring balance into the atmosphere for the benefit of humankind. Agnihotra Yainya has its origin in what is known as the Veda. The word Veda comes from the Sanskrit root VID, which means to know.

The Veda are similar in foundation to the 42 Books of Djehuty. Djehuty represents the divine principles of knowledge, wisdom, science measures, laws, geography, architecture, astronomy and all aspects of governance in the arts and sciences for the building and maintenance of MAATIC civilizations.

Therefore, the Khamitik equivalent or translation for the fire purification aspects of the Veda or the Agnihotra fire rituals are linked as follows: In Hindu the term Agni means Fire Deity or God; Hotra is the process of purification rituals. In the ancient Khamitik language of the Mdw Neter-words of Mother Father of creation and nature- Agni relates to Sekhmet the feminine principle of fire, healing and purification; Rerit is an Mdw Neter term meaning Fire Goddess; Hotra is linked to the Mdw Neter term of Het Heru meaning the house of the sun and fire. Rekhit is the Mdw Neter term along with Rekhiu, which are terms for fire goddesses.

It is significant to mention here that Rekhit is the link phonetically to the Japanese word Reiki. This represents fire within healing hands and touch, in the Khamitik language. Knowledge and evidence of ancient wisdom implies that the word Reiki was re-discovered from the ancient practices of Khamitik civilizations, as demonstrated on the walls of the great pyramids today.

Origins of the fire for purification in Khamitik language of the Mdw Neter: Links the practices of the Agnihotra fire healing ritual to the origin of man and woman,

Khamit. Allow this information to resonate, vibrate and communicate through you!

The Ntrt divine feminine principle of Sekhemet is personified as the element of fire in states of purification for cleansing, destruction of negative vibrations, and healing. Sekhemet represents heat and the protective powers of nature. Sekhemet carries the divine and dual energy of heaping and destruction reflected within nature that is mirrored within our human body temple.

In ancient Khamit the origin of using the fire as part of the offerings comes from how fire was used by humans to satisfy the digestive system. By observing nature we saw that by making offerings to ancestral deities in respect to the voice and other offerings documented on Ancestral sacred temples, all fire rituals were used to purify physical food offerings. Very similar to the Spiritual offerings used by lighting incense to purify the atmosphere, integrating rites of earth fire and air with water into balance. It all goes back to a solar ritual of giving reverence to Ra as the sun by replicating the ancestral fire as an ancient ritual of having the fire rise to the heavens. These teachings have been shared with me for the purpose of sharing the ancient knowledge with you directly from Per Ankh 101 and the Seneb Djesek 203 course in heal yourself: the element of fire published in 2002. Mer

Veda means pure knowledge in the Sanskrit language. In ancient Khamitik temples it is written as the philosophy of enlightenment and higher wisdom. This knowledge was given at the time of creation for all of humanity. Therefore, the process of VedaNta is universal. It is essential to all of humanity, irrespective of race, creed, color, religion or country. Imagine having knowledge that is vast as the ocean, wide as the sea and permeates throughout the entire universe. Agnihotra Therapy is the science of bioenergetics, psychotherapy, medicine, agriculture, biogenetics, and climate engineering. This meditation ritual is a sacred purification process for the atmosphere, with elements from the earth of copper shaped into a pyramid turned up to the biorhythms of the endocrine system, the earth and the energy from the sun. Organic Cow Dung is used as a pure burning agent for the ritual. Natural Ghee butter is the sweet elixir that is used to pour onto the cow dung for igniting the fire. Brown rice is the grain that is used for pouring prayers and vocal toning into the atmosphere. I was first introduced to this ritual in 1993 by a member of an Agnihotra community in Baltimore MD. My personal Journey into Inner Peace lead me one evening into a room filled with quietist, preparing for what I later learned to be the Agnihotra Fire Mediation. The fire is laced with a powerful aroma of the soothing essence of cow dung and natural ghee butter and rice. Who would have ever thought that cow dung could be such a sweet healing agent for the earth, the atmosphere and the human emotions? During the ritual, I became overwhelmed with a feeling of joy and inner peace at the depth of my soul. I was overwhelmed by a powerful since of unconditional love, deep silence, serenity and community support. I literally did not want to leave that space. The joy, love and inner peace was like a very strong magnet that was holding me down in absolute divinity. The people that were the keepers of the fire were sincere with pure hearts, dedicated to healing the earth and its atmosphere at every nano-pore of the universe. Learn more about how to practice the Agnihotra Fire Meditation and help save the planet by cleaning the ozone layer, purifying the atmosphere through the scientific use of fire. Visit:

www.Agnihotraindia.com

A Brief Sample of how to Perform the Agnihotra Fire Meditation Ritual

According to the organization Agnihotraindia.com

Be sure to check your local sunrise and sunset timetable schedule for ritual accuracy. Place a few pieces (5-8), of the Cow Dung cakes in the Agnihotra pot. Now melt the natural ghee and soak a piece of the cow dung, camphor or a cotton wick with the ghee. Arrange the remaining pieces of dung around the soaked dung neatly. Use a matchbox with sticks to light the fire. Watch very closely and blow on the fire gently if needed to increase the blaze. Take two pinch full's of clean, unbroken rice grains (raw) on your left palm or in a small glass or clay pot. Smear the rice grains with a few drops of the natural ghee. Divide the ghee soaked rice grains into two parts. Just as soon as the clock strikes the exact sunrise/sunset time, start to offer one part of the rice to the fire in the pot. This is the time that you begin to chant the Veda mantra. While making your offering of the rice to the fire you repeat "Svaha", each time that you pour the rice into the fire. The Agnihotra Fire Meditation Ritual is a very specific and sacred process that must be studied thoroughly before practicing.

Visit: www.agnihotraindia.com for more details and specific instructions on how to perform the Agnihotra Fire Mediation Ritual.

Chakra Meditations

To conduct a successful Chakra Meditation, it is essential that you have a clear understanding of how to visualize the location, color and sound associated with the chakra within your body. All of this information has been given to you in earlier chapters of this book. Before practicing this meditation, I recommend that you revisit those chapters and use the chakra chart with the detailed information on it while practicing this exercise.

Locate a comfortable place and position to sit in for the Chakra Meditation. Decide on a particular aroma (essential oil) or a selection of essential oils to treat the room with before your begin. You can practice this meditation in the silence or with synergy music to enhance your experience. It is your choice. As you begin to go within, taking deep cleansing breaths; begin to focus your attention on one chakra affirmation at a time, as you allow an image of the chakra to appear in your mind's eye. Once you feel a connection with the flow of your meditation, begin to repeat to yourself in the silence or out loud the associated chakra affirmation. For example, you would focus your mental attention on the root chakra and visualize the color red, sound in the key of C and use the essential oil sandalwood for the Sensorium Sound Meditation™. Use your Key Master to determine the musical key note for this meditation. This meditation can also be practiced one chakra at a time. If you have a specific need that is associated with only one of the chakras, you can conduct this meditation with that one chakra only if you desire.

Affirmations for Healing the Endocrine System

A Sensorium Sound Meditation™

ROOT

I am rooted and grounded to be stable, safe and secure.

SACRAL

I am empowered to create and transform.

SOLAR PLXUS

I am energized with personal power; I release fear
and replace it with thoughts that strengthen me.

HEART

I am an open channel for divine love,
compassion and unconditional love.

THROAT

I am free to speak boldly what I think and feel.

THIRD EYE

I am attuned for intuition and
insight with inner guidance.

CROWN

I am one with God and all creation, and
connected to the divine mind.

Meditation Ritual Treatments for Healing

There are five basic meditation treatments for health and healing

The Meditation Ritual Treatments for Healing are practices on how to tune into universal life force energy. Universal life force energy can be incomprehensible, yet every living being is receiving its gifts every day, consciously and unconsciously. Be aware of the power of the one Supreme Being. It is the absolute infinite loving energy that gives us life and breath. IT IS THE KEY TO ACCESSING THE WISDOM HEALING POWER OF life force energy. The Divine is unseen spiritual vibration that awaits our willingness to become aware of it, accept it and use it for giving life. Universal Life force energy is ready and available to all who are seeking and have a sincere desire to learn the art of spiritual healing.

I first became aware of this energy as a young child. I didn't really know the true source or even the purpose of it, but I knew that there was a higher power, an unknown energy force that could be tapped into and used for life purposes. As I grew into woman hood, I remember being challenged with the discomforts of stress and physical tension. I sought many ways to release these sensations in order to find inner peace and emotional balance. I prayed for God to help me find a solution. My spiritual solution came while jogging one morning in my neighborhood while living in Atlanta Georgia. I had become exhausted and decided to take a rest on the side of the road near a private lake. The rays of the sun were bright and strong while the air was cool and brisk. I lay down by the side of the lake and closed my eyes. The sun's rays were caressing my face and I felt the warmth of the suns energy penetrating my entire body. I rested until I felt that it was time to leave, but as I made the effort to move, I suddenly felt a powerful presence come over me and my thoughts started racing inside of my head. I felt that my spirit was being given a divine message that said, "Come closer, come a little closer to God," said the inner voice, adding, "do not be afraid, trust in your mind and heart". I awoke from the trance I was in and concluded that I had just had a talk with God by the lake. Since then, I began to have many moments of silent, spiritual connections and conversations with God. The body will always respond to the mind's command.

Whatever your mind tells your body, your body response will do it. I began to tell my body to relax and release the pain, and surely, gradually, with a sense of unawareness,

I was one day without emotional stress and physical body tension. My curiosities about this natural healing process lead me to discover Transcendental Meditation. My teacher, Mama Paulette Bell, was my first life coach instructor, mentor and spiritual director from the time I was thirteen years old. After years of serving as a psychotherapist and healer of my own life's negatives, I discovered some basic meditation treatments that work instantly when applied properly with regularity. The following meditation rituals are designed for personal meditation that can be practiced anywhere at any time.

Meditate on Holy Things

Meditation # 1 Total Body Relaxation

This meditation Ritual starts with identifying a sacred space to meditate. Select a meditation CD with very little musical distractions, something like a chant or drone music in the key of G. I suggest that you use the **Sound Vibornics™ Sonic Stress Reduction CD** for this ritual. (See the resource guide in the back of this book) Prepare your aromatherapy diffuser with an essential oil blend of lavender (5 drops), eucalyptus (3 drops) and one (1) drop of peppermint. Place a yoga mat or rug on the floor with a blue candle on the front center of the mat. Be sure that the candle is safely secured and in a glass container. Lie on the mat or rug on your back. Place a small pillow under your knees to support your lower back. You may also have a small pillow to rest your head on if you desire. Always begin each meditation with 3 to 10 deep cleansing breaths.

Instruction #1 ~ Scan your body mentally very slowly from the tip of your toes to the center of your crown chakra, located at the top center of your head. Become aware of any discomforts, tension, stress or obstruction in any part of the body. For assisting your scanning exercise, you may visualize the cells, blood veins and muscles of your body, as you scan from your feet to your head.

Instruction # 2 ~ After you have completed the scan, keep a mental note of where you felt the tension and return to those places one at a time.

Instruction # 3 ~ When you return to the places that you felt need more attention, embrace those areas with your hands. Focus your meditation on healing and relaxing the areas with your thoughts. Embrace the tension with your inner voice and speak to your body messages of love and gratitude. Thank your feet for taking you every place you have even been, thank your heart for pumping just the right amount of blood into your system for life, thank your eyes and ears for serving you etc. Get to know your body so that it will respond to your relaxation commands at any time.

Instruction # 4 ~ Each time that you command a part of your body to relax, become aware of the tension leaving your body and a total sense of relaxation taking over.

Instruction #5 ~ Closing the meditation begins with stretching your legs with a pointed toe. (Left leg first and then right leg). Raise your left arm into the air and stretch upward and then stretch the right arm. Repeat this exercise three times. Then slowly roll-on your side and lift

yourself up by supporting your body with your hands &
arms onto your knees and then get up.

As you think, so you are, as you
continue to think, so you remain

Meditation # 2 Quieting the Mind

The practice of purifying the mind and letting go of those
thoughts that cause suffering and emotional pain in our
lives is a worthwhile skill to acquire. Before you begin
this meditation, take several slow, deep cleansing breaths.
Hold your body erect while sitting in an upright chair
or on the floor. After you have taken at least four deep
breaths, begin to allow your breathing to become normal
again. At this time, many thoughts will come and attempt
to distract your attention in the mind.

Do not focus or dwell on those thoughts, good or even
bad, just begin to become aware of the thoughts as you
are mindful of them passing through your mind. Let
your thoughts come and go without getting involved in
the details or even trying to suppress them, just allow it
to happen. Watch your thoughts passing through your
mind as if you are watching them on a movie screen. In
this Meditation Ritual, you become the mirror reflecting
the solution of your own problems without stressing the
mind. The human mind has absolute freedom within

its true nature; it is your conscious thoughts that create mental congestion, confusion and dis-stress. You can attain this freedom with your pure intention to let go and quiet the mind. You do not have to work towards this goal; just allow the practice itself to take you into a quiet mind for healing.

Instruction #1 ~ Practice this meditation ritual in the morning or in the evening. With consistent practice you will begin to realize that your mental congestion is passing away and you're intuitive knowing and ability to find creativity and mental freedom is increasing.

Instruction #2 ~ Make a clear intention to practice this Ritual everyday for the purpose of relieving the mind from mental congestion, confusion and the inability to concentrate.

Instruction #3 ~ Your meditation space must be clean and free from all distractions.

Instruction #4 ~ Wear loose clothing and preferably no shoes during your meditation.

Instruction #5 ~ Sit on a cushion in the lotus position/ or with your legs crossed in a comfortable position. Keep your back straight.

Instruction #6 ~ Place your tongue at the roof of your

mouth at the place where your teeth and upper roof meet and then close your mouth.

Instruction #7 ~ Close your eyes slightly while focusing in a downward position take deep breaths through the nostrils and exhale through the nostrils.

Instruction #8 ~ Follow the meditation instructions given in the introduction of this Meditation ritual.

Instruction #9 ~ Practice is the key!!! This ritual will generate positive energy, power and insight. Let go of the need to know how long or when this will be achieved, just become one with the practice and it shall be.

Fear........ It is only a mind state

Anxiety..... is the result of unfinished business and self doubt to finish it

Resentment ......is the result of self doubt

Meditation # 3 Power of the Mind

Cleansing the Consciousness of Resentment, Fear and Anxiety

Resentment is a feeling of indignant displeasure or persistent ill will at something or someone regarded as wrong. Fear is an unpleasant often strong emotion caused by anticipation or awareness of danger, a reason for alarm. Anxiety is a painful or apprehensive uneasiness of mind over an impending or anticipated ill, fearful concern or interest. Together these emotions bring physical discomfort; emotional trauma and worrying about life. Consciousness is the quality or state of being mentally aware, with a keen awareness of something within oneself. It is an upper level of mental life, which a person is aware of most often unconsciously. A person who has attained an enlightened consciousness is a person who has attained a higher level of life awareness. A highly evolved and enlightened person has learned to master the **Power of the Mind**. "The universe is mental and all is in the mind". Cleansing is intended to refer to the practice of eradicating whatever is obstructive, thwarting or degrading….. to get rid of impurities…to cleanse, to purify, to free from guilt or moral blemish….to become pure or clean.

Release Me

This is the time to release;

To breathe

To breathe deep

To breathe deep without trying to breathe

To think about no thing

To rest and release and breathe

Your eyes will clean with tears

Your body will rest its aches

Your mind will forget time

Your spirit will remember its birth

Release and Rest …….. Written by BaBa Akili

Instruction #1 ~ Create an alter space for meditation and prayer in your home, in the woods, in your yard, or wherever you feel that the sprit is leading you to practice this meditation ritual.

Instruction #2 ~ It is suggested that you use fresh flowers, a 7 day white candle in a glass and place them in a significant place on the altar.

Instruction #3 ~ **Smudge** the space with the sacred smoke of Frankincense and Myrrh resins. Sprinkle Florida Water in all corners of the room or in a circle surrounding your alter space.

Instruction #4 ~ **Take** a spiritual cleansing bath. Clean the tub out with peroxide after each bathing experience. A spiritual bath can help to work out negative emotions or bad vibes. The results will be peaceful balance in your entire life. It is recommended to take a spiritual bath whenever you need emotional balance and cleansing of negative **EMOTIONS**.

a. Take a peppermint soap shower before taking the spiritual bath to clean the body.

b. Run warm to hot water in the tub with four cups of Sea Salt.

c. After the tub is full, pour one box of baking soda into the water.

d. Optional to put aloe vera natural bubbles or 12 drops of lavender essential oils in the bath water.

e. Do not put any toxic chemicals in the bath water.

f. Light a white candle and place it in front of you on the bath tub if possible.

g. Look deep into the flame and visualize the energy from the flame surrounding your entire body. This flame symbolizes the voice of God.

Take in the message (s) that will be given to you during the bath from the voice of God. With the intention of Cleansing the Consciousness of Resentment, Fear and Anxiety ask yourself the following questions;

• Where is resentment in my life?

• Where is fear in my life?

• Where is anxiety in my life?

h. When you have completed the spiritual bath, unplug the drain and wait until all of the water has drained out before getting out of the tub. Pat dry and put on comfortable clothing. (WARNING…. be mindful not to fall asleep. If you have a tendency to fall asleep in meditation or while taking a hot bath, remember to let someone know what you are doing and check in with them when you have completed the exercise)

i. Drink an 8 oz. glass of spring water with lemon after the bath meditation ritual is complete.

j. Remember that this entire exercise is the meditation ritual, so maintain a meditative mind and heart during the entire exercise.

Instruction #5 ~ Write down any thoughts or messages that you received during the mediation in your journal in the back of this book. If you feel that no messages came to you, write about that and continue to conduct the meditation ritual and notice how your experience will become clearer as you practice more and more.

Remember to keep your intentions of cleansing in mind during the entire mediation ritual.

The body knows more than a fearful, doubtful mind

Meditation # 4 Visualizing Wholeness

Releasing emotional pain, and eliminating self doubt

Visualization is the formation of mental images or the process of interpreting in visual terms a mental, emotional or physical intention. Wholeness is the completion or totality of something or someone in their fullest nature or development. Visualizing wholeness is the ability to interpret in mental terms the intention of complete fullness in life. The mind instructs the body on what to do, when and how to do it. If you can visualize yourself in a peaceful place, near the ocean on a clear sunny day, you can actually create a relaxation response in the body. The brain does not know the difference between reality and imagery. This being the case, you can create your own physical reality by visualizing it and telling the body to eliminate all other interpretations of it. Emotional energy is a state of feeling, a psychic and physical reaction in the body. Emotion is subjectively experienced as strong feelings and physiologically involving changes that prepare the body for immediate vigorous action. (The definitions of Visualizing, Wholeness and Emotions have been taken from the Webster's Ninth New Collegiate Dictionary). Throughout life, we are often challenged by self doubt and emotional discomfort. The Meditation Ritual for

Visualizing Wholeness brings a total sense of balance and emotional strength to the seeker. It is our thoughts that tend to hold us back from realizing our true greatness and fulfilling our purpose in life. The thoughts are centered in the consciousness of mental energy. Therefore, to realize a Vision of Wholeness, we must create a language for *Negative Thought Stopping.*

VISUALIZING WHOLENESS
ELIMINATING EMOTIONAL PAIN AND SELF DOUBT

Instruction #1 ~ Place four drops of Patchouli and Rose essential oils in an aroma diffuser or on a piece of cotton cloth.

Instruction # 2 ~ Sit in an upright position in a chair or on a floor mat with the cloth in the palm of your hands. Be mindful not to inhale the cloth too closely to your face or get the oil in your eyes.

Instruction #3 ~ Take 10 deep cleansing breaths through the nostrils to the count of five. Inhale five counts, exhale five counts. Then take five deep releasing breaths. Inhale through the nostrils and exhale through the mouth with the sound of ahhhhh, do this five times.

Instruction #4 ~ Repeat numbers 2 and 3.

Instruction #5 ~ **Focus** your attention on the center of your forehead and begin to pay attention to your thoughts. Remember to relax your shoulders and lower back during this Ritual. When you notice a negative thought, tell the thought to stop with your mind and gently return your attention to your forehead.

Instruction #6 ~ Once you feel that the thoughts are no longer racing and filling your mind with negativity or worry, command your mind to visualize an image of you happy and totally content with yourself without Self Doubt or emotional pain. See yourself free of whatever appears to hold you back emotionally. Release all doubt that this is not possible. Just for this meditation Ritual, see yourself completely whole and free of all emotional pain or any negative condition that your mind may be focused on. See yourself doing what you desire in your heart to do in life. Resist the urge to tell yourself "this is not possible, or I cannot do this". If these thoughts come into your mind, use the thought stopping technique and continue your visualization. Tell yourself to STOP the thought that you no longer want to focus on. This is the practice of thought stopping. Practice visualizing in your mind's eye an image of you completely whole and free of all emotional pain or self doubt. Accept this as your reality in your feeling world. Become aware of what this feels like and allow your visualization to serve as a movie of your life free, realizing the emotional, spiritual and physical reality you desire in your life.

Instruction # 7~ Visualize yourself doing things that you would not normally due because of self doubt and emotional pain. Visualize yourself talking to someone that you find it difficult to talk to in your life such as a parent, your boss, a husband, girlfriend etc. Tell them everything that you have always wanted to say. When you see that person in your vision make sure that they are aware that you are speaking to them and do not give them permission to speak in your visualization. You are in control of this visualization conversation.

Instruction #8 ~ It is recommended that you practice this meditation ritual whenever you feel the need or until you no longer have feelings of self doubt or emotional pain.

In your mind's eye, in your heart center and in your emotional consciousness, see yourself whole, emotionally free and feeling the Love.

Meditation purifies the mind..... Practice
the power of compassionate mindfulness

Meditation # 5 Omnipotence of God
(Releasing the power of your higher self)
"Becoming.... right before your very eyes"

Did you know that there is a presence that watches over you at all times? The omnipotence of God is the most awesome experience that anyone could ever know. This power is often times referred to as the Higher Self. Have you ever been involved in a situation that you thought had no way out or possible solution?, and suddenly, just in the nick of time, you had just what was needed? This experience is known as Divine Intervention and/or the Omnipotence of God. This is an unfailing source of divine love, inner guidance, inspiration and eternal spiritual energy. Releasing the power of your Higher Self is a gradual meditation process that is connecting you with the Divine Mind, Subtle Body Energy and your Divine Nature. When you connect with your Higher Self, it will help you solve life problems, offer guidance on soul purpose and support your destiny in life. Your Higher Self has always been with you throughout eternity. If this presence is unknown to you, you can take the time to re-connect and your consciousness will always be adjoined with the Omnipotence of God.

The first step into unfolding your Higher Self is the power of **I AM**. The phrase **I AM** is God's name in man and woman. It is the true spiritual self referring to the ideal that we are made in God's own image and likeness. The **I Am** presence is the manifestation of creating a sacred union between the spirit, wisdom, love, inner peace, power, emotional strength and truth.

- The **I AM** presence is the Kingdom of the Heaven within us.

- The I **AM** presence is the metaphysical representation of the spiritual self.

- The term **Christ** is the scriptural name for the spiritual **I AM.**

- The **I Am** presence in each individual is the will in its highest form.

- The **I AM** Presence and the Christ Self combined, is referred to as the Higher Self.

- The Christ consciousness is the mediator between God and man.

- **Christ** in the Webster's Ninth New Collegiate Dictionary is defined as an "ideal type of humanity".

The Christ or perfect womb man concept is referred to as the Divine Mind, the true spiritual Higher Self. **The presence of I AM is an innate knowing of the truth deep within you. It resides in each one of us, and waits on you to call it fourth.** As your mind concentrates on the Omnipotent Power of God, the I **AM** is called on, and all you have to do is behold the wonders through your mind's eye, your emotional consciousness and your heart center. The possibility of healing is manifested through the quickening power of the spoken word of God. The word of God **(Truth)** is the creative energy with the potential of obtaining all of God's healing attributes.

The Meditation Ritual of the Omnipotence of God is the creation of a new state of consciousness. Discovering an understanding of God as a Spirit Consciousness, and your relations with God as a Spiritual being. The Omnipotence of God is a mental perception, which requires a specific process of inner development before it becomes a part of your conscious knowing. The heart of man is the true temple of God, the natural church of worship.

Willingness to enter into the True Temple of God opens the passageway into the Spirit of Truth.

INTRINSIC BONDING WITH GOD MEDITATION RITUAL

To prepare for this meditation, it is suggested that you sit in the room with your alter. Light a white candle and place it on your alter and light a jasmine stick of incense. You may also use frankincense and myrrh. Be sure that the incense that you use is made with pure essential oils. Allow the aroma to permeate the room before you begin. You may also use an essential oil in a diffuser or by placing four drops of the oil on the floor, or rug in front of you. It is not necessary to do this each time that you practice this meditation. The meditation can be practiced anywhere that you desire and at any time with or without the aroma. The aroma helps to support the meditation experience and prepare your mind for relaxation and connection with the Most High God.

Instruction #1 ~ The first process of going inward begins with the silence. The silence is waiting for you to enter into it and find comfort and rest. Begin to take deep breaths (follow the deep breathing exercise instructions). The silence is a state of stillness of thought, body and mind.

Instruction #2 ~ Relax your body. Release the hold on your shoulders, neck, facial muscles, upper chest, lower back, thighs, knees, calves and feet.

Instruction #3 ~ Anoint your head with olive oil. (Olive oil is symbolic of the Holy Spirit, peace and love.) (Bless the olive oil yourself or ask your spiritual leader to anoint it for you. Keep the oil on your alter at all times.)

Instruction #4 ~ Allow your mind to gently focus on the idea of Gods Omnipresence.

The power of unlimited authority and influence, present in all places at all times, an awesome concept to behold.

Instruction #5 ~ Become aware of the idea that your mind can connect with the Divine mind of God. Evoke the secret place of the most high and just know that God creates by the power of his word. Meditate on the phrase, "God said...and it was so."

Instruction #6 ~ Concentrate on the idea that all in harmonies of the world can be eradicated from the earth by eliminating them from the mind of man.

Instruction #7 ~ There is no reality of the existence of in harmonies within the Divine Mind. It is a manifestation of man, and has no real substance in the Mind of God. There is only harmony and oneness with the Divine Mind.

Instruction #8 ~ The Divine Mind manifests into reality with thought through ideas of good intention. Become aware of the Divine good that God has in mind for you to manifest.

Instruction #9 ~ Within the Divine mind all things are possible. All ideas are created by the Divine mind of God. May thy will be done.

Instruction #10 ~ Meditate on the idea that the Kingdom of God is within you. The Kingdom of heavenly ideas comes from the intentional adjustment of your thoughts from lack, doubt and fear, to wholeness, truth, light, love and divine order. Creating a knowing deep within you that all is in divine order, and all is well with my soul.

Instruction #11 ~ Eliminate all thoughts of in harmony from your consciousness and connect with the Divine Mind with the intention of receiving divine ideas.

Be willing to change your thought patterns to integrate with divine thought patterns.......

And in time "Ye Shall Be Transformed".

Instruction #12 ~ To close this meditation ritual, slowly allow your awareness to return into the room. Become aware of your fingers, toes, shoulders, arms and legs. Move your fingers and toes and take deep breaths. Upon your third deep breath begin to slowly open your eyes, blinking them two to three times before opening your eyes completely. Give thanks and praise for the healing experience.

Create your own Spiritual Life Support Group

CHAPTER SIX

Serenity Living

Lifestyle Support Therapy

You have engaged upon the dawning of a new lifestyle. This lifestyle is composed of serenity living, movement, meditation, affirmation, emotional freedom and prayer, as part of your daily regimen. While in the process of creating your new lifestyle, it will be good to begin practicing various types of support therapies that will enhance your Serenity Life experience. Lifestyle Support Therapy is an opportunity to maintain your serenity and inner peace with various forms of the healing arts. Lifestyle Support Therapy is focused on creating sacred space for healing and using relaxation, meditation, prayer and other forms of the healing arts as a major approach to personal transformation, discovering soul purpose in life and understanding the Power of the Mind as the gateway to the kingdom of HEAVEN.

We understand that all causation in the world is mental, and that all of our affairs of mind and body; jobs, businesses, home life, relationships, health and all of life experiences are manifestations of our own mental states of awareness and consciousness. Creating a sacred space for healing will support you to find peace of mind, mental clarity, prosperity, freedom from life's pain and suffering through mastery of the Art of Serenity Living and mastering the Art of Being.

LAUGHTER: To laugh and release tension with laughter is a life giving experience. The act of laughter involves movement of the facial muscles, the diaphragm, endorphins and stimulated blood circulation. Laughter provides all of the ingredients required for improved optimal health.

SOUL THERAPY: Soul Therapy sessions take you to a new place of clarity and feeling of lightness, inner peace and relaxation. Sessions are focused on where you want to be in life and offers transformation of thoughts, feelings, emotions and misbelief's in life. Each soul enters this earth with a purpose and mission….. Soul Therapy is a process for discovering that purpose and opens the passage way to begin living out your life mission by re-patterning negative thought energy into positive thought forms.

Anyone at anytime in their life can benefit from the experience of Soul Therapy. Any thought that one is having constantly, or randomly which cause sadness, anger, confusion, loneliness, feelings of abandonment, or just nervous anxious feelings can be cleared during a series of healing sessions. All issues & misunderstandings, whatever they look like or sound like are energy patterns which have been collected throughout our lives. These distracting thought patterns drain vital life force energy and may eventually create physical disease or illness. Releasing thought patterns which have manifested as habitual ways of being will result in a feeling of physical lightness, mental clarity and emotional freedom. Each session is a unique experience, guided by your soul and supported by intuitive healing and holistic treatment modalities. Through the use of Aromatherapy, Rieki, Reflexology, Hypnotherapy, Sensorium Meditation, Synergy Music, Spiritual Baths, Angel Healing Harps and more. You are gently guided on your journey to mental clarity and personal fulfillment in life. Soul Therapy is getting to the core issues underneath the blocks in your life.

Moving Forward

TRANSFORMATIVE SONIC ALIGNMENT: (TSA)
A Full Body Meditation Treatment designed to create an instant shift in consciousness. Improve your focus, clear mental congestion, release stress and reach deep, deep levels of relaxation. The Full Body Sonic Meditation is a vibrational healing treatment designed to recondition the

mind for affirmative thought; releasing the tendency to think negatively and replacing it with positive attraction. The Full Body Sonic Meditation is a deep relaxation and chakra healing treatment designed to strengthening the aura with sound vibrational frequencies. The Sonic Meditation resonates every cell, every organ and brain wave functioning within the entire body. The Sonic Meditation allows you to experience the oneness of everything around you, touching the 5 senses and activating the 6th sense. The Full Body Meditation activates the etheric integration of the body, mind and spirit into pure light. Consciousness becomes extremely heightened, clear and focused in a way that you have never experienced before. Being open to the healing energy of Transformative Alignment allows time to stay with the energy for long periods of time after each session. For the fullest impact of the TSA, become an observer of your own state of being and see who you really are. This deep level of relaxation allows the body to release stress and pain, creating a total sense of harmony, balance and clarity.

MASSAGE THERAPY: Deep Tissue and therapeutic massage promotes relaxation, helps to relieve stress and energy imbalances. Schedule a full body massage with aromatherapy oils on a regular basis. Massage creates a deep sense of relaxation and is stimulating to the central nervous system while increasing blood circulation. It affects the nerves, organs, muscles, glands, circulation and aids in the release of toxins. There are various types of massage techniques available for healing such as; Swedish massage, deep muscle, relaxing and others.

Locate a massage therapist that makes home visits, and enjoy the healing energy of massage in the comfort of your own living space.

SILENCE: Quiet your mind with silence and deep rhythmic breathing exercises for tissue oxygen building. The silence is a powerful place to go for wisdom, clarity and peace of mind. Often it can be challenging to find the silence if you live a very hectic lifestyle, or if you are unable to quiet your mind do to consistent worry, anxiety or stress. Do not be discouraged if you cannot find silence, if you sit with it long enough, it will find you. Contact Serenity Healing Arts and attend the Journey to the Higher Self Silent Retreat to learn more about accessing the silence. The healing is in the silence.

REST AND RELAXATION: Create a rest and relaxation period in your daily, weekly, monthly regimen. This should be with no interruptions. Plan regular weekend getaways to places where you can get close to nature and the water for healing. I recommend that you visit www. heavenhouseretreat.com, located in Berkeley Springs West Virginia, for a pure experience of total rest and relaxation.

At the Heaven House you will be my guest in a lovely luxury mountain home. Plan a personal healing retreat with me at the Heaven House and your soul will never forget it.

SOUND THERAPY: Listen to soft healing music and the healing tones of singing crystal bowls. The crystal bowls offer a peaceful and deep relaxation experience. Sound therapy is a form of vibrational medicine. This is based on the concept that illness or dis-ease is characterized by blockages in the central nervous system, arteries and veins. The high vibrational frequencies of the crystal singing bowls has the power to induce brain wave activity that create frequencies designed to reduce stress, relive pain and release illness. Consistent exposure to these sound frequencies can promote homeostasis in the body, mind and spirit.

BRIEF VACTIONS: At least once a month plan a inner peace getaway vacation. Even if you just travel on a train to nowhere all day and night, drive to the mountains or ocean shore. Go somewhere to get away from the same environment you live and work in daily. Locate local state parks with cabins to rent. Contact your favorite airlines and search for specials on the Internet. Visit our travel web site and book a mini vacation.

ACUPUNCTURE: An ancient medical practice which

uses micro needle insertion as the method for releasing pressure and energy that causes dis-ease in the body-mind-spirit. You can now have choice with needless acupuncture. Acupuncture is a part of Chinese medicine. It is thousands of years old and is often used with herbal medicine, relaxation techniques and massage therapy. The practitioner inserts very tiny needles at key points along the body that are connected to the organs and affects the entire physiology of body functioning. Acupuncture stimulates natural pain killers called endorphins and serves as an antidepressant effect on the emotions. Acupuncture is a major healing process which can improve lung functioning, boosts the immune system, illuminate emotional and physical pain.

HYPNOTHERAPY: Experience a deep state of relaxation and focused concentration while being guided into inner peace and resolution of past traumas that hold you back in life. By the use of gentle non invasive suggestions, you can realize effective behavioral changes that will improve the quality of your life. Hypnotherapy opens the door into significant insights about eating disorders, smoking, negative habits, relationships, weight gain, weight loss and encouraged healing of the mind, body and spirit. You can learn self strategies to reach deep, deep levels of relaxation.

COLON CLEANSING/COLONIC IRRIGATION:
Gentle internal cleansing of the colon using warm filtered water to remove accumulated waste, toxins and gas. Colon therapy is a practice of gently washing the entire colon of accumulated wastes and detoxification of the entire body system. The colonic machine provides a passageway for the inflow of water and the out flow of fecal matter and other toxic materials found in the colon. You will notice an immediate sense of high energy and lightness of the mind and body. Colonic therapy is effective with eliminating headaches and nervous tension.

REFLEXOLOGY: A hands on technique used to facilitate healing and balancing of the body organs by applying compressed pressure to the nerve endings on the feet and hands. Reflexology releases tension in the body and improves nerve and blood supply to the brain. It is the study of behavior as a series of reflexes in the central nervous system. Reflex is an involuntary action in direct response to a stimulation of nerve cells. Reflexology massage techniques stimulate an impulse process which causes a autonomic nerve response and increased blood circulation. These impulses travel along a nerve canal to the spinal cord relaying a message to relax the muscle. Reflexology relieves tension and stress from the body while supporting the state of homeostasis for the entire body.

REIKI: An ancient Laying on the Hands spiritual healing technique used for stress reduction and relaxation to balance mind, body and spirit. Reiki is a gentle, subtle healing of a spiritual nature. It is simply a transmission of divine love from one soul to another. The power of touch always results into a deep feeling of connectedness and a sense of emotional wholeness. Reiki is known to have roots in the ancient Egyptian and Tibetan traditions, later rediscovered by Japanese culture and coined as the word Rei-Ki, pronounced Ray-Key. In the ancient Egyptian tradition, it is known to have been pronounced Ra-Ka, which is phonetically pronounced Rey-Key.

The word Reiki means universal life force energy. It is considered to be the essence in life which all matter is created. The ancient teachings of Egyptian philosophy tells us that this source of life force energy Rey-Key, flows through all living things. It connects us to the very nature of the air, the water, the tress, the animals, the earth, the stars, the heavens, the spirit of man and woman. Reiki holds the key that sparks the healing energy that flows through the body, mind and spirit. It is a powerful presence that generates radiating heat wave energy from the hands, and can be felt inches away from the body. The process of Reiki allows the receiver to feel warmth and healing energy wherever it is needed, and it allows the giver the opportunity to express unconditional love while communing with the spirit of man and woman.

DIET THERAPY: Increase protein and mineral intake. Eat vegetables (raw and steamed), soy foods, sprouts, B-vitamin rich foods, brown rice, and green vegetables high in magnesium and use good food combining. Reduce caffeine and sugar intake, no liquids with meals and do not eat and run, watch T.V. or while working. Make smoothies with, organic royal flaxseed, royal jelly and ginseng. Drink Aloe Vera Gel Juice and slippery elm. Exercise daily with some form of aerobic exercise. Drink lots of fresh clean water all day.

HERBAL & VITAMIN THERAPY: Explore the many varieties of powerful multi-vitamins, gingko, licorice elixir, calcium, magnesium. Begin to stock your medicine cabinet with natural tonic herbs to take the place of toxic medicines. Consult a doctor before starting any herbal regimen, particularly if you have an existing health challenge. Every home should have the following natural herbal tonics: Garlic, Echinacea, cayenne, gingerroot, milk thistle, peppermint. Remember that herbal remedies can very seriously contra interact with prescription drugs.

EARLY MORNING AROMATHERAPY
MEDITATION BATH (5:00AM)

Sometimes when you awake in the morning, the body and mind is not connecting well, and you may feel a slight headache or body ache and need a boost. Take an early morning aromatherapy bath with Valor essential oil blend, made by Young Living Oils, with four cups of Epsom salt. The Valor therapeutic blend pursues a sacred physical and spiritual connection with the emotions and offers an increased sense of strength, self-esteem, and courage. This is a great way to release the morning blues, and open the heart for the dawning of a new day. Peace is with you.

CALMING HERBAL THERAPY: Ingredients: Valerian Root, Kava Kava, Chamomile tea, Homeopathic tinctures for nerves, sleepy tea. Bach Flower Essences, Liquid Photo-Caps by GAIA HERBS; Migra-Profen offers the ultimate support during stress and tension, GAIA HERBS KAVA KAVA Liquid Photo-Caps; for the ultimate support for relaxation, GAIA HERBS Serenity Liquid Photo-Caps; for the ultimate support for relaxation. GAIA HERBS Echinacea, Golden Seal, and Propolis Supreme throat spray for supporting the throat chakra and expressing the will.

The sister's with Ivy at the Sweat Lodge Smudging Ritual

The Native American Sweat Lodge:

The sweat lodge is a sacred spiritual ceremony for physical, mental, emotional and spiritual purification. Participants come to pray and connect to creator (in very personalized and special ways each person believes in). They also come to seek guidance for important questions, and to ask for healing in the body, mind, emotions and spirit for self and others. The ceremony integrates the four fundamental elements of fire, wood, water and stones, which are also called river rocks. The sweat lodge ceremony is conducted in the darkness of an enclosed structure made of natural materials designed in the shape of a dome, representing the womb. The river rocks, affectionately known as grandfathers, are heated in an outside fire and brought in symbolic numbers into the lodge and placed in a central pit inside of the lodge. The pit is a large hole that can hold up to 30-35 river rocks. The rocks are heated in a specially made fire bed for 3 hours or until the rocks are glowing red embers. Water poured over the rocks induces sweating and releasing of toxins in the body, mind and spirit. During the ceremony, there are four basic sacred herbs that are used during the process: sage, sweet grass, cedar and tobacco. The ceremony consists of four rounds of prayer, which involves singing, praying and sharing of stories. Native American drums and rattles are often used in the lodge during the singing and prayers. Between the rounds of prayer, the door is opened and participants may take a brief break, as the rocks and water are being prepared for the next round. As a sacked ceremony, all that transpires in the lodge is left there and not shared with anyone that is not in attendance of the ceremony. The Traditional Native American Sweat Lodge ceremony is a very powerful healing experience and should only be performed by a trained authentic facilitator, given permission by the elders.

AROMATHERAPY FOR STRESS RELIEF:

Ingredients: Lavender oil, Chamomile oil, Ylang Ylang oil, Neroli oil, Juniper Berry oil. Apply pure essential oils topically to create a sense of total wellness for the mind, body and spirit. The purest oils on the market today are manufactured by doTerra Essential Oils. Do Terra Living produces essential oils that will soothe the senses, invigorate the body and promote physical well-being. Essential oils in the purest form can be used in the following ways—www.mydoterra.com/serenityhealingarts

1. Stimulating the immune system.

2. As an anti-viral, anti-microbial, anti-tumoral, anti-fungal, anti-bacterial.

3. Anti-oxidant Stimuli

4. Increasing cellular oxygen

5. Detoxifying cells and blood in the body

6. Creating harmony to the emotions

7. Encourages balance to the body

8. Encourages stress release

9. and much, much more

EPSOM SALT BATHS: It is not recommended to take salt baths if you are challenged with high blood pressure. Before trying a salt based bath treatment, consult with your physician first. If you have any medical conditions that could be contra to using salt, do not practice this ritual. An Epsom Salt bath is an extremely powerful source of cleaning through the skin. Epsom salt is best known for its soaking aid for minor sprains and bruises; however, it is also an effective saline laxative. The laxative effect can be achieved by taking the Epsom salt internally or soaking in up to 8 pounds of the salt in a regular sized bath tub. The Epsom salt increases water in the intestine thereby promoting bowel movement and the release of toxic waste. By soaking the body in the correct amount of Epsom salt, the same effect can be achieved. For soaking away aches and pains, it is normal to use 4 to 6 cups of Epsom salt per one gallon of water, to achieve good benefits.

Epsom salt should only be used as an occasional laxative. Prolong use may result in serious side effects. This treatment should not be used for children. Epsom salt baths can help improve sleeping disorders when used minutes before retiring for the evening. Epsom salt baths are refreshing and can help one sleep well though the night awakening in the morning with a fresh attitude and energized for the day.

CASTOR OIL PACK: The castor oil pack is made from multiple layers of white wool flannel, folded to fit the area of the abdomen. The flannel is saturated with a high grade cold-pressed castor oil and then placed primarily on the right side of the abdomen and covered with plastic. Once the pack is in place, a warm moisture heating pad is placed over the plastic and secured with a towel or blanket to hold it in place. The treatment should take no longer that one hour. I like to warm the oil before saturating the flannel. This is very relaxing and a highly effective technique for detoxification. The castor oil pack helps to stimulate the liver and colon, and is a great combination with an internal cleanse program. Using the castor oil pack treatment is good for increasing lymphatic fluid flow. After the treatment is completed, the skin should be cleaned with a special solution such as baking soda and water or an alkaline formula for cleansing skin such as CASTOR WASH by Baar. Before you try a castor oil self treatment, it is highly recommended that you research the process first, or go to a professional for the service. I find the castor oil pack treatment to be very healing when I am not feeling good in general. It offers a sense of wellness and a feeling that healing is taking place faster. For more information on castor oil read **The Edgar Cayce Handbook for Health through Drugless Therapy** by Harold Reilly and Ruth Hagy Brod, (Virginia Beach, VA: A.R.E. Press, 1975)

TEA THERAPY: Relaxing with a cup of tea is a simple, easy and powerful technique for nourishing the body, mind and spirit. Peppermint and chamomile tea are my recommended teas of choice. New research indicates that green tea is good for health. Green tea comes from the leaf of the shrub. Select teas that are loose or packed in organic tea bags. It is good to do something special for yourself by taking a cup of relaxation tea while sitting back to contemplate, concentrate, meditate and pray.

- Steep your tea for 3 to 5 minutes releasing the highest level of antioxidants.

- Purchase a traditional tea set to add to the ambiance of tea time for relaxation.

- Plan a relaxation tea gathering and invite friends to enjoy tea together.

- Purchase a variety of herbal teas and locate a special place in your kitchen to keep them handy.

- Take a tea time kit to work with you; include the following teas; chamomile, peppermint, ginger, green, jasmine, honey, white china tea cup with dish.

- Take a trip to your local Chinese tea shop and select special relaxation teas for your home tea collection.

For the true tea lover, the following Tea Terms are offered to describe the various tea flavors that one can experience:

Bright: A cup of tea that sparks with energy and is void of dullness.

Body: A tea combination filled with fullness and strength, a full taste of distinction.

Burnt: Exposed to extremely high temperatures during boiling.

Flat: Lacking a light briskness after standing for long periods of time in the water or on the shelf.

Dull: Exposed to bacterial contamination, improper boiling or excessive moisture.

Full: A perfect cup of tea endowed with strength, flavor and body.

Create a Sacred Tea Experience with Your Friends

Serenity Wellness Living Serenity Wellness Living Serenity Wellness Living Serenity Wellness Living Serenity Wellness Living Serenity Wellness Living

Journey into Inner Peace Serenity Living

Take the time to make your home a Serenity Living Home environment, a place where you can find refuge and personal healing. You want a place that others can feel the healing energy as soon as they enter your space. The **Serenity Living Model** consists of warm and energetic colors, water fountains, aromatics, green foliage (live plants and flowers), comfortable furniture, ambient lighting, decorative room themes, natural textures and natural light. If you do not have the luxury of enhancing your entire living space, select a room or a corner that will be dedicated to **Serenity Living**. Your Serenity Wellness Space should be designed to support relaxation, meditation and improved emotional and physical health. **Serenity Living** depends on a personal commitment to rest, relaxation, hydration, oxygenation and good nutrition. Spend some time in your favorite book store and select various inspirational decorating magazines to get you started. For example find a magazine on ideas for great lighting, paint colors, and room themes. Study furniture stores and magazine covers to get some ideas of how to begin. Decide on what mood you would like your space to create.

Structural Elements for Creating Serenity Living

- ❖ Color for influencing environmental attitude
- ❖ Aroma for establishing energetic qualities
- ❖ Music for mood enhancing
- ❖ Cultural designs for image and cultural identity empowerment

The Psychology of Color for Serenity Living

Colors are linked with our moods and state of mind. Study the energetic influences of color and select color themes based on your personal needs. Reds, oranges and yellow are warm and expansive colors. Yellow walls encourage the ideas of flow, and softness. They tend also to generate excitement and joy. Blues, indigos and purples are calming and cooling. Soft hues of Purple represent spiritual healing and serenity. Strong rich hues of purple give an impression of luxury, power and royalty. Shades of gold encourage a feeling of groundedness, loyalty and trust. Selecting colors for carpet is a special art for enhancing the **mood ~ tude** of your serenity living space. The psychology of color is a spiritual language that can be learned with focused attention and intent. You can find a limitless amount of information on the internet, or if you choose, locate a really good book that explains the power and healing energy of color. When you are able to comprehend and truly understand the power of color in the human psyche, you can create a relaxing, wellness living environment anywhere.

Effective application of color can add life and energy to any environment and work space. Transfer your Serenity Wellness Living **mood ~ tude** into your work environment. If you cannot paint your office, use textures and color with pictures, special lighting, green foliage, colorful space rugs, wall fabric hangings, aroma and other creative ways to establish color energy in the room.

Aromatherapy Energy Engineering

Aroma Energy Engineering with aromatherapy is another powerful way to encourage inner peace and emotional balance in your home and work environment. Smells affect the way you feel emotionally and physically. Have you ever walked into a room and smelled something that reminded you of your grandmother's love, and recall that feeling? Or a memory of a smell that made you sick, and begin to feel sick or nauseous? Aromas affect energy and emotional levels of reaction and response. Aromatherapy can be used in your living space to cleanse and purify the air thereby encouraging wellness and optimal health. There are various ways in which you can apply aromatherapy (Essential Oils) in your **Serenity Living** space:

- Vaporizers
- Diffusers
- Droppers
- Scented Candles
- Scented Flowers
- Room Treatment Resins

Inhalations can be used very effectively to treat physical and mental conditions. 5-10 drops of the appropriate essential oil blend can be used. Inhalation therapy is effective due to the fact that essential oils are highly volatile and easily diffused into the air for treatment. There are four basic approaches to inhalation therapy:

1. The hot water method – produces steam for lungs, sinus and throat.

2. Ambient room diffusion – Which affects mood, and can be used to influence the mental state. (use aroma therapy diffuser or potpourri burning pot)

3. Inhaling Oils – place a few drops directly onto a handkerchief, cloth or your hands. A few drops can be placed on your pillow, bed or rug. Just be creative.

4. Use a total of 6-10 drops of essential oils, added just before getting into the tub. Relax 15-20 minutes. Soak long enough for the oils to enter the pores in the body.

Music Medicine for Serenity Living

Music, sound and vibration have the ability to make profound changes in body chemistry. The brain responds to sound and vibration affecting hormone levels. Sound and vibration can even strengthen the immune system; reduce anxiety, tension and stress. It can also decrease high blood pressure and encourage happiness and emotional balance. Correct selections of music can set the **Tone-Mood** for gatherings, private inner peace time, meditation, yoga, exercise, bath interludes, family meetings, cooking etc. You should make music and sound a significant part of your life every day, on every occasion. Creating the **Tone- Mood** in your home or work space will make a tremendous difference in your life, as well as in the life of your house guests, family and friends.

Designs and Image Engineering

A major component to creating Serenity Wellness Living, is the image that your space projects. Creating serene images that promote cultural identity within your living space is empowering. While attending a conference tour in Senegal, West Afrika, I spent twelve days in the Afrikan community and experienced traditional Afrikan living. The experience made me keenly aware of the energies found within Afrikan spirituality and the importance of using those elements to create sacred space. The creative genius of the traditional people in various villages I visited continues to provide me with spiritual inspiration. The use of handmade objects using the soil from various regions in Afrikan continent; the many textures of the wood, the colorful fabrics and natural textures can provide an authentic traditional experience in your living space.

Your environment interprets your level of consciousness. Look around your living space right now, and become aware of the level of consciousness that your image is projecting. You can also conduct this survey in your work environment. Decide on what image and energetic qualities that you would like to express and get busy creating them. Have fun doing it!

Wellness Living with Intent

You must create a wellness environment in order to reap the benefits of optimal health. Wellness living requires the creation of a new lifestyle. Creating life practices that support, inner peace, emotional balance, happiness and love is the primary objective of Serenity Wellness Living. A home should offer safety, security, and a total sense of comfort and satisfaction. Your commitment to creating a Serenity Lifestyle encourages self love and self determination.

Intentional Rest & Relaxation is also an essential component to Serenity Living. Your environment must be arranged to encourage and promote rest and relaxation. Reduce stress, tension and anxiety with a good quality mattress for sleeping. Comfortable bed linens, pillows and lighting should be chosen for the maximum comfort they will provide in your sleeping space. Limit as many distractions in your sleeping space as possible that could disrupt your sleep pattern.

Your Serenity Living Wellness Environment requires time and effort to engineer. If you live in a rural area and have access to good spring or well water, you are way ahead of the program. Most of us are living in metropolitan areas that have treated water regulated by city municipalities. Careful attention to filtering your water and air will help promote total wellness. Sophisticated water and air systems would be the ideal approach to protecting the quality of the water and air in your home; however, I realize that this may not be a realistic option for some. However, I encourage you to do some research to discover alternative ways of improving the air and water in your living and working space.

Air purification is another major component to serene living. Pollution, dust, mold and mildew are difficult, but possible to remove from the home. Diffusing essential oils that are designed to purify the air should be used daily. The use of a shower water system will also help to remove chemicals, including chlorine from your shower & bath experience. Doterra oils produce an aroma blend called purify, which is designed to detoxify airborne pollutants.

HEALING TOOLS THAT ARE A MUST HAVE
ON THE JOURNEY INTO INNER PEACE

*Create a Sacred Healing
Sanctuary in Your Home*

Relaxation can be a learning experience with dedicated practice. Relaxation techniques are natural tools for influencing the process of spiritual, emotional, mental and physical awareness. With practice, relaxation will reduce fatigue and better enable you to handle life circumstances. Relaxation techniques will not eliminate all causes of stress and tension; however, it does eliminate with faithful practice the symptoms (ex. shallowness of breath, muscular tension, eye strain, headaches etc.) and offers the necessary tools to strengthen your potential of successfully handling daily stress.

The more you practice, the more relaxation becomes natural; it will become a lifestyle and emotional attitude for the rest of your life.

The following healing tools are a must have in the home of Serenity Lifestyle Living.

Aromatherapy: Body, Face, and /or scalp massage products that assist in improving circulation through use of aromatic essential oils extracted from plants, trees, and flowers.

Loofah Sponge: A natural sponge used for scrub/ exfoliation. The Loofah sponge is an invigorating, deep cleansing body treatment, which improves circulation by exfoliating dead skin cells and nourishing the skin.

Deluxe Slumber Spa Set: The Slumber Spa Set is used to create the perfect sleeping environment for relaxation and release of fatigue. You can create your Slumber Spa by purchasing a body pillow, soft aromatherapy eye mask that completely filters light. Select your favorite color for the benefit of color therapy. I have two Slumber Spa Kits laced with lavender and ylang ylang, one is blue and the other is purple. To accompany your eye mask, include a set of reusable earplugs to help block out distracting noises like snoring, phones and people talking while you are trying to rest.

Spa Stone: Natural lava rock pumice defoliator. This lava rock defoliates and smoothes rough skin. The lava rock is used for the hands, feet and body. The lava rock gently smoothes away the feeling of being rough and raggedy physically and emotionally. The lava energy serves as a symbol of renewal.

Bath Tub Head Rest: Collect a variety of bath tub head rests. Look for plastic, terry cloth and foam head rests to create different bath experiences.

Extra large Bath Towels: Collect a variety of extra large bath towels in different colors. For a special touch, have your name embroidered onto the towels for those special bath Interludes. You can also name the towels based on your favorite baths, such as; Serenity Morning Bath, Spiritual Bath, Relaxation, etc. You can purchase specialized bath towels by visiting: www.serenityhealingarts.com

Cleansing Enema Kit: An at home colonic irrigation treatment. This is used for washing out of the bowel by gentle enema, a liquid injected through the anus that stimulates evacuation of toxic waste in the body, mental clarity and emotional calmness.

Neti Pot or Sinus Rinse: A gentle, effective nasal irrigation system. Helps relieve sinus congestion, post nasal drip, nagging coughs and sinus headaches. Just add a pinch of sea salt with warm water and rinse your nasal cavity clean.

Body Fat Analyzer and Scale: Measures body fat percentage and weight.

OM Tuning Fork: Tune your body, mind and spirit with the OM tuning fork. It is tuned to the OM vibration and can be placed directly on the body for physical and spiritual attuning. It is also a great meditation tool. The OM tuning fork is capable of relieving tensed muscles and creating a relaxed mood.

Solar Harmonic Healing Tuning Kit: A whole body tuning kit designed to balance and harmonize the chakras. With practice you will become familiar with the sonic communication patterns of the tones, and develop the capacity to create the same vibrations during meditation and as a response for healing the central nervous system.

Shirodhara Kit: A traditional Ayurvedic treatment that pours warm oil across the forehead and into the scalp. A deep healing and relaxation experience, which helps to reduce tension, enhance blood circulation, and is known to help improve the memory. The oil helps to aid in nourishing the hair and scalp. This classic Ayurevedic treatment traditionally comes with a copper bowl, pouring pot, copper rings, copper stand, oak base and copper polish.

Steamy Wonder Spa Kit: This spa kit turns your massage table into a steam spa experience. It is a very lightweight fabric canopy with Velcro strips to seal the edges. In just a few moments, the steam generator produces a healing steam creating a table top sauna in your home. The kit includes a digital thermometer, circulation fan and instruction manual. The Steamy Wonder Spa portable steam sauna is an environmentally friendly system that is useful for anyone looking for the health benefits associated with a steam sauna. Some of these benefits include relief from joint pain and muscle soreness, improved circulation, reduced inflammation, and relief from allergies and asthma. Aside from the health benefits, the Steamy Wonder Spa also serves as a beauty aid with benefits such as weight loss due to detoxification, beautiful skin, and cellulite reduction.

Paraffin Wax: Warm wax brushed over the body, feet and hands which is then wrapped up to perspire in order to draw out toxins, cleans pores and softens the skin. The heat and wax emollient instantly soften the skin and soothes aching muscles and relieves tension. The wax can be purchased in various calming aromatherapy scents. My favorite is lavender and mango.

Dead Sea Salt: A cleansing treatment used to remove dead skin and improve circulation by rubbing a mixture of coarse salt and aromatic oils on the body. Blend the salt with African Shea butter to sooth and soften calluses. Drops of essential oils may be added to the salt to create an aromatherapy scrub treatment.

Skin Brushing: The skin is the largest organ in the body, and the largest area toxins are eliminated by. Use a brush with natural bristles. Brushing the skin improves circulation of blood and lymph functioning. Brush from your feet to your head.

Epsom Salt Bath: Eliminates built up stress. Take the time to take an Epsom Salt Bath to control tension and stress. Create the mood with candles, aroma and no interruptions. (Use 7-16 pounds of salt in a hot tub of water. The temperature should be comfortable to sit it. (Avoid this ritual if you have high blood pressure.)

Meditation Music: Collect CD's of relaxation music. Purchase synergy music for meditation produced by Ivy. Practice the Sensorium™ Sound Meditation Method daily, with music. Ask your local music store to order Ivy's Meditation Music if you do not see it in your favorite store.

Aromatherapy Facials: Cleansing masks, facial toners, essential oil conditioners, essential oil treatments, and Queen Afua's green clay. To purchase aromatherapy become a member of the do TERRA Living aromatherapy family. doTERRA has the most purest essential oils in the industry. Visit my website and order today. www. mydoterra.com/serenityhealingarts

Aromatherapy Candles: Select authentic aroma candles by checking the ingredients. Jasmine, Lavender, Grapefruit, Meditation, Lemon, Eucalyptus, Peppermint just to name a few, are good ones to have all of the time in your home. Look for hand poured bee's wax candles for a more natural soothing experience.

Massage Tools: Electrical vibrational massage tools are great for relieving stress and relaxing tensed muscles. Look for the dual pivoting heads with dual speeds with heat and contour capacity. Body sticks are great hand held tools that can be used anywhere at any time for stress relief.

Chi Machine: A lymphatic and circulatory stimulator that oxygenates the system. One treatment instantly provides deep relaxation, and rejuvenation. The vibrational therapeutic motion generates healing benefits for the entire body.

Shiatsu Massage Cushion: The shiatsu massage cushion uses a moving mechanism that helps knead away aches and pains by traveling up and down the back and neck.

Body Masseur Massage Mat: This is a full body mat with an effective massage tracking action. You can use this mat to massage your body from the head to the feet. Look for a body mat with heating action to help relieve stiffness and tension in the body.

Reflexology Foot Machine: Soothes and relaxes tired feet with a vibrational massage action that relaxes the entire body.

Moist Heat Electrical Pad: Produces intense moist heat for pain relief. Look for the heating pad with programmable digital hand control for selecting the best temperature at your fingertips.

Aromatherapy Diffuser: There are various types of diffusers for your use. The most inexpensive are clay potpourri pots with tea light candles. Pour a little water in the pot and up to 10 drops of essential oils. The most effective and enjoyable one that I have found is the doTERRA LOTUS DIFFUSER. The Lotus diffuser uses a highly efficient real time atomization technology to effectively diffuse essential oils into the environment. The essential oils are atomized into minute ion particles and active oxygen ions, which are more easily absorbed by the human body than oils diffused by conventional diffusers. doTERRA is pleased to be the exclusive distributor of the Lotus diffuser to you and your family. www.mydoterra.com/serenityhealingarts

Herbal Teas: Look for teas that have no caffeine in them. Stock sleepy time; tension tamer, eye bright, chamomile, and peppermint tea in your kitchen cabinet, and office.

Aromatherapy Paraffin/Beeswax Ear Candles: Ear Candling relieves sinus pressure, eases ear aches and is a very relaxing treatment. Ear candling is a centuries old technique. The treatment can be used to relax tension and soften the heart center. Ear candling comes from the traditions of the Egyptians and Native American cultures.

Hot Stone Massage Kit: Relieves tension, stress and fatigue. Using the hot stone therapy technique is easy; however, you can have better results if someone does it for you. It is a wonderful exchange opportunity for you and a friend. The hot stone massage is an extremely effective way to create harmony, initiate positive energy flow and promote a calming sense of emotional balance.

Serenity Aroma Living

Living a Serenity Aroma Lifestyle ensures a personal commitment to experiencing the life enhancing benefits of therapeutic grade essential oils. According to doTERRA, essential oils are natural aromatic compounds found in the seeds, bark, stems, roots, flowers, and other parts of plants. They can be both beautifully and powerfully fragrant. If you have ever enjoyed the gift of a rose, a walk by a field of lavender, or the smell of freshly cut mint, you have experienced the aromatic qualities of essential oils. Essential oils can lift the mood, calm the senses, and elicit powerful emotional responses felt deeply within the soul.

doTERRA states that essential oils have been used throughout history in many cultures for their medicinal and therapeutic benefits. Modern trends towards more holistic approaches to self care and growing scientific validation of alternative health practices are driving a rediscovery of the profound health benefits of essential oils. Many have powerful cleansing properties and are naturally antimicrobial. Their unique chemical structure allows the oils to pass directly through the skin for immediate systematic responses to topical application. Specific oils have been identified as dietary aids to promote vitality and wellbeing. Essential oils play a vital role in my life, and I want to share this Serenity Aroma Lifestyle with you, for your Journey into Inner Peace.

Aromatherapy Therapeutic Singles

Balance the Body, Mind, and Spirit

Essential Oil	Therapeutic Benefits
Basil	Depression, anxiety, brain & memory
Geranium	Depression, anxiety, skin conditions
Patchouli	Confusion, indecision, apathy, depression
Ylang Ylang	Calming, aphrodisiac, anger
Pine	Calming, muscles relaxant, lungs
Lavender	Calming, stress release, meditation, lungs, burns
Chamomile	Calming, migraine headaches, tension, relaxation
Neroli	Soothing, relaxing

Rose	Depression, love, nervous tension, relationships
Sandalwood	Relaxing, sedative, depression relief
Basil	Valued for its restorative and calming properties. Soothing sore muscles and joints, ease breathing, and is cooling for skin.

Ivy's Favorite Essential Oils & Blends

Do TERRA Essential Oils are the highest grade of oils on the market today

Breath Respiratory Blend	Respiratory relief and soothing effect. Breath easier. Pleasant aroma creating a calming sensation and restful sleep at night.
Sandalwood	Supports nerve function. Promotes emotional well-being
Lavender	Supports the immune system. Calming, relaxation and emotional balance. Maintains healthy lung functions.
Eucalyptus	Support respiratory system. Evokes feeling of emotional security and a feeling of well-being.

Purify Cleansing Blend	Helps to cleanse and purify the air. Calming for good sleep. Eradicates unpleasant odors.
Balance	Promotes balanced energies in the body. Emotional empowerment, confidence and feelings of self-esteem.
Elevation	A joyful blend to elevate the mood.
Peppermint	Supports digestion, healthy lung function and restores mental alertness, especially for fatigue.
Rosemary	Promotes blood circulation and healthy lung function. Improves mental clarity and resolves feelings of grief and loss.
doTERRA Essential Oils	ARoMATOUCH TECHNIQUE A Clinical Approach to Essential Oil Application
Blue Chamomile	Deep relaxation and feelings of total well-being.

Patchouli	Increases sexual desire. Very calming for the nervous system and supports positive attitudes.
Serenity Calming Blend	Gently sooths away tension and promotes total well-being.
DigestZen	Restore normal balance to digestive system.
Slim & Sassy Metabolic Blend	Helps manage hunger, calm the stomach, and lifts the mood. Drink between health meals.
Balance Grounding Blend	Creates a sense of calm and well-being. Relieving the feeling of disconnectedness or anxiety.
Young Living Oils	Rain Drop Therapy Technique Warm drops of essential oils down the spine with moist heat.

All products of doTERRA Essential Care

www.mydoterra.com/serenityheaalingarts

When using oils for massage or placing them on the body, you must always dilute the oil with sunflower, almond, grape seed or jojoba oil. You may want to experiment and blend several varieties together to learn which one works best for you.

My favorite starter kit for aromatherapy is the ***doTERRA Introduction to Essential Oils Kit***. doTERRA Oils are high grade therapeutic essential oils. The starter kit offers a great opportunity to try the most popular essential oils on the market. The following details the healing qualities of the oils in the Kit: (This information has been taken from research and documents published by doTERRA Oils and Young Living Products)

Lavender – is the most versatile of all essential oils and has been highly regarded as soothing to the emotions, spirit and skin. Research has proven that lavender can increase the healing process of burns. The French scientist Rene' Gattefosse was the first to discover these properties when he severely burned his arm in a laboratory accident. It can be used not only for burns, it can also be used to cleanse cuts, bruises, scrapes, and skin irritations. Lavender has also been studied for its relaxing effects, both physically and emotionally.

- Apply to the bottom of feet or on a pillow before sleeping

- Use to calm reaction to a bee sting or bug bite

- Use with bath salts for a relaxing spa bathing experience

- Apply to wrists or inhale when traveling to ease motion upset

- Use with peppermint for a healthy scalp massage

- Add to lotion for a stress-relieving hand massage

Lemon – is bactericidal and helps activate the white corpuscles of the immune system, according to Jean Valnet, M.D. It is antiseptic and anti-parasitic. It can serve as an insect repellent.

- Add a drop to a water bottle

- Diffuse aromatically or apply topically for mood elevation

- Add to drop of honey to sooth a cough or sore throat

- Add to olive oil for a non toxic furniture polish

- Add a drop of lemon and peppermint to your toothbrush after use

Peppermint - Soothing for the digestive system. Dr. Valet, M.D. studies peppermints ability to affect the liver and body respiration. Scientists have also researched peppermint's role in affecting impaired taste and smell and mental accuracy when inhaled.

- Rub on stomach or feet, or take one drop internally to calm indigestion or upset stomach
- Use with lemon in water for a healthy, refreshing mouth rinse
- Apply with lavender to sore, tired muscles and joints
- Breath during a meal to help you feel full
- Use with lavender and lemon during allergy season
- Add to shampoo and conditioner for a stimulating hair and scalp massage

Aromatherapy Baths & Shower Steam Recipes

A Stimulating Bath

Peppermint oil 3 drops
Rosemary oil 4 drops
Juniper oil 4 drops

A Calming Evening Bath

Lavender 4 drops
Marjoram 4 drops
One capful of sesame seed oil

Depression Relief- Harmony

Jasmine 10 drops
Relieves depression.
Creates a calm atmosphere.
Aids in fear and emotional suffering.
Address low self confidence and
Relieves menstrual pain

Harmonizing

Sandalwood 15 drops
Lavender 20 drops
Harmonizing, calming tendency.
Quiets emotional volatility.
Relieves tension and anxiety.
Aids in sleeping and releasing stress.

Aura Strengthening Healing

Lavender 15 drops
Roman Chamomile 5 drops

strengthens the heart beat and
Stimulates overall wellness.
Relieves pain, physical and emotional discomfort.

Mental Stimulation
Eucalyptus 20 drops
Basil 8 drops
Lemon 5 drops
Encourages mental stimulation
Increasing concentration
Balancing & releasing emotional overload
Good for asthma, bronchitis, sinus problems and sore muscles

Powerful Heart Tonic
Lemon Balm stimulates red & white blood formation
Stimulates the body's immune system
Energizes the morning blues
Purifies the air.

Joint & Muscle Pain
Thyme 5 drops
Juniper Berries 8 drops
Wintergreen 5 drops
Dead Sea Salt 4 cups
Relax muscles and relieve aching joints.

Holistic Detox
Green Tea 4 tea bags
Milk Thistle 2 tea bags
Rosemary 10 drops
Dead Sea Salt 4 cups
Soak the tea bags in the hot bath water

While taking the bath. This bath helps to purify the system and protect against toxins.

Cold Symptoms & Flu Relief
Echinacea & Golden Seal 4 tea bags
Eucalyptus 10 drops
Dead Sea Salt 4 cups
Soak tea bag in the hot bath water while
taking the bath. This bath helps to relieve symptoms of a cold or flu. Eucalyptus, thyme, tea tree and peppermint are anti-viral and help calm symptoms of sinus congestion.

Instructions for Creating a Steam Shower
In order to create a steam shower experience, use the same essential oil combinations indicated for each bath by dropping the oils in the middle of the bath tub after you have turned the shower on, and the water is comfortably hot. Just carefully step into the bathtub and inhale the vapor steam of the essential oils before you take your shower. You can create the mood that you desire by selecting the proper combination of essential oils. For example, to energize, you may want to use a combination of lemongrass and lavender to get you started in the morning. Become creative with the ideas and you will soon be enjoying aromatherapy showers. You can also purchase an essential oil bath salt shower head from Young Living Oils.

NOTE: Enhancing Your Bath Experience
To add an extra ounce of enjoyment to your bath experience, you can always add one box of baking soda

and ½ cup of sea salt. This will add a rich quality to the water and increase the healing values of the bath.

Go into the River and Heal

Ivy's Favorite Aromatherapy Relaxation Bath Products

The Healing Garden	Lavender therapy body soak & shower Gel
Apothecary	Spa Sea Salts
AHAVA Essential Dead Sea Treatments	Dead Sea Mineral Mud & Mineral Salts
Booth's Mineral Bath Soak	Mint & Lavender
EQ Essential Oil Products	Bath Suds, Shower Gel & Body lotion
OLBAS Herbal Therapeutic	Herbal Bath

BATHERAPY Natural Mineral Bath & Liquid Suds	Bathe Away Aches and Pain Lavender & Mint
Epsom Salt & Baking Soda	Blended with eucalyptus & lavender
Rite Aid Therapeutic Soaking Aid	Dr. Teal's Epsom Salt Lavender/Peppermint Soak Solution

You can blend different essential oils to make your own bath combinations. Always note (safety precautions) never put pure essential oils directly onto your skin. Always dilute with carrier oil, or water to be safe. Purchase the doTERRA book on aroma therapy to learn more about the use of essential oils. Visit the doTERRA website: to purchase essentials oils on line. You will have the purest oils on the market mailed directly to your home. Call 1.800 411.8151 for more information. Use ID # 58363 to place your order. You can also go to the website at www. mydoterra.com/serenityhealingarts to read about essential oils and how to purchase them.

Meditation with Essential Oils

Rub the essential oils onto the body, specifically in the areas of the energy centers or chakras. Write down your feelings about your experience in your Meditation Journal located in the back of this book. This is a good way to learn about the energetic qualities of the oils and their mood altering and healing effects for you. Once you get a feeling for the oils, blending them will become a creative art experience, and you will learn the true essence of each oil and how they work together for wellness. You may want to experiment with the oils to see what combinations you prefer.

Before you begin your exploration with the essential oils for meditation, it is recommended that you conduct an isolated area skin test. If you are not sure about the level of sensitivity that you may have to the oils, you can place a small drop on your arms or leg and watch it closely for about one hour. If you notice that the area turns red or irritated with any level of discomfort, then you may be experiencing an allergic reaction. If this is the case, you must discontinue the use of the oil immediately, and consult your primary health care provider. Be very mindful of the oils once they are placed in your hands. The oils are highly concentrated and will irritate your eyes. If the oils should get into your eyes, immediately begin to wash your eyes out with cold water, until the sensation is relieved.

To begin your meditation with essential oils, you can use a diffuser, cloth, tissue, vaporizer, or humidifier to emit the oils into the air. The diffuser is the simplest technique to fill the air with the aroma for meditation. The diffuser will disperse the essential oils into what is known as a micro-mist. This essence mist can last for hours in the air of the room, in some cases it can even last for days. The mist also serves as a powerful disinfectant for bacteria, fungus and mold. This practice is considered to serve as an anti-bacterial and anti-viral process. The use of essential oils with a light consistency is recommended. I learned this lesson by placing patchouli in my new diffuser, and found that it clogged the system. It took me days to clean it out well enough to use again because of the thickness of the oil. After that experience the diffuser never did work well for me.

Meditation with essential oils can be a very rewarding experience. I have noticed that when I am conducting a private or group meditation, the outcomes are very different when I do not use essential oils. I have learned that the meditation with the essential oils is always a more profound experience for deeper levels of relaxation and stress release. Meditation without essential oils is less stimulating and allows for a more subtle meditation experience. Both techniques are effective to use.

Using the vaporizer or humidifier is a very stimulating experience as well. The vaporizer and humidifier approach to using essential oils is a convenient technique if you do not own an oil diffuser. Just add 6-10 drops of doTERRA essential oils in the cool vaporizer or humidifier and wait a few minutes for the mist to permeate the room. In the case of congestion, it is good to use eucalyptus and peppermint oil in the vaporizer. This will help relieve the congestion and restore nasal breathing. The breath is a powerful tool in the process of meditation. The vaporizer technique will offer a better opportunity for deeper and clearer breathing during the meditation experience. For the most effective experience I highly recommend that you use the doTERRA Lotus Diffuser. When I am conducting a Meditation, it always begins with the treatment of the room. You can treat the rug and the four corners of the room with essential oils. Simply place two to three drops of your meditation essential oil in the four corners of the room at lease five minutes before the meditation. While lighting your meditation candle, you can add to the strength of the aroma by dropping the oil into the candle wax. This is a very easy way to create your own aromatherapy candles. This really ensures that you have authentic oils in your candle. It also helps to create a wonderful candle experience for meditation.

Outdoor meditations can start by, treating the ground with Florida Water and Lavender essential oils. Florida Water is a clean smelling cologne for external use only, by Murray & Lanneon. It is used for purifying the air during spiritual ceremonies. This is a very powerful meditation because the essences blend with the earth, and Mother Nature is being nurtured. It is a great idea to sprinkle the Florida Water in a circle which surrounds the area that you plan to meditate in. In other words, you should sit in the middle of the circle after the area has been treated. The circle should be wide enough to accommodate the number of people expected to participate in the mediation. It is also a good practice to treat the area designated for meditation, before anyone else enters the area. This practice gives you the opportunity to send prayers and set the tone for the meditation without distractions or disruption. Now, you are ready for meditation with essential oils.

Sacred Home Relaxation & Serenity Ideas

How often do you take time to get away and relax, de-stress or go on a journey for inner peace? In today's society, our lifestyles are moving so fast that we seldom realize that we are stressed or even worse, dis-stressed. We can easily use the excuse that "I do not have time", or "Where will I get the money?", "I can't just take time out for myself". I have learned that these excuses can possibly shorten your life on earth. The faster we are hurry in life, the faster we are ensuring the end of true living and maybe even precious life itself. In my holistic psychotherapy practice, I find myself giving instructions to clients on how to create their own personal healing retreat at home in order to make progress. You do not have to spend hundreds of dollars to find inner peace. This is one of the very few things in life that really can be free, or experienced with very little expense. What you really need is a will to live, a desire for inner peace and the willingness to do something about it. Creating a positive leisure experience for *you* is one of the healthiest gifts that one can give to oneself.

Taking time for personal relaxation and serenity ideas is an effective way to eliminate the symptoms of a pressurized daily lifestyle.

Take a long, reflective look at your life right now!................ Write in your journal everything that you see that takes up most of your time. This includes daily chores, family responsibilities, how much time you spend at work, on toxic relationships etc. Write the key words that describe how you feel about it. Be mindful to do this with honesty. This is your very own private personal life assessment, and no one else can see it unless you reveal it. Now, take a long reflective look at what you do on a regular basis for fun, relaxation and enjoyment!..................

Write in your journal everything that comes to your mind, including key words that describe how you feel about it. Now you must review your lists and make a determination on what you will eliminate from your life and what you will keep. Now be aware that this exercise may bring up certain people in your life that are no longer serving your *highest* good. Do not be surprised if some of those images are the closest people to you, including family members. This brings up the issue of deciding what stays and what goes. You may not be able or want to rid yourself of family members, but you can decide how much influence and regularity they will have in your life, especially during your relaxation and serenity time. I pray that you have decided that you are worthy of serenity, relaxation and inner peace. It is time to release and let go. If you must get back to the pressurized world, at lease take some time for yourself to create wellness and optimal health at home on the weekend, so that you will have more energy to cope and continue to live with ease. You can create your own private retreat right at home.

First, make the decision to spend an entire weekend with private time for personal healing. Clean your home thoroughly. If you can, hire a house keeping service to clean your home for you. I often do this for myself, when I return it's not only refreshing but an emotional healing experience as well.

Make sure that you have all you might need for the weekend so you won't have to leave the house. Change the message on your answering machine to this; "Hello, I have taken a Personal Retreat for myself by myself in my own home for the entire weekend. I am taking the time to rejuvenate, relax and create a refuge of inner peace. I really would love to talk with you, so please leave a brief detailed message, and just as soon as my healing time is over, I will reach back out to you. Thank you for allowing me the time to take care of myself"…..Beep. If you live with other people or have children in your home, write them a letter in preparation for your personal healing retreat. Talk with your family and explain the need for everyone to take the retreat with you. Should you experience some resistance, make some decisions about how to resolve the differences and move forward with your experience of inner peace. This same approach is true for young mothers or mothers with young children. If you cannot find or do not have someone to care for your children during this time, allow the children to experience the inner peace with you. If you have some resistance to believing that this is possible for you, remove that thought and allow yourself the opportunity to try. If you can find just several hours of inner peace, that is a great start! Just get started. I have provided for you some ideas on how to plan your weekend. These are just a few ideas to get you started. Be creative and come up with your own activities or non activities if you wish. You will be happier with yourself after you experience taking control of your life for creating inner peace.

PLAN A DETOXING WEEKEND

1. Create a light salad candle light dinner. Prepare a healthy smoothie or tea therapy combination and sit back to enjoy. Place blue candles on the dinner table with classical music in the background to complete a perfect evening.

2. Take a Personal Spa Day. Select an exclusive Hotel Spa and make reservations for an entire day. Select you're spa treatments in an order that will give you time in between each session. Plan to arrive about an hour before your first treatment and have a light lunch or breakfast in the hotel. Drive up to the lobby driveway and ask for valet parking. After you have had lunch, sign into the Spa and prepare for a day of total relaxation, inner peace and emotional release. If you can, you may want to make reservations to spend the night and transform your Spa Day into a relaxing, luxurious night. Enjoy!

3. If finances are a concern, don't let the idea of your personal Spa Day go. Call your local recreation center and find a community indoor swimming pool with a jet spa and or sauna. This generally will cost you anywhere from $5-$10 a visit. You deserve it, so get it going.

4. Create a Personal Home Spa Day. Select the special spa treatments that you would like to experience and prepare them in the bathroom. For example, you may decide to take a paraffin wax and hot rock massage treatment, or an Epsom salt bah with an ice glass of lime water.

Be creative and make sure that there will be no interruptions during this special time.

5. Make live fruit and vegetable juices for breakfast, lunch and dinner.

6. Choose the toxic relationships that you need to release and work on the plan to release them. If you feel that this is not possible, at least choose to leave these people out of your detoxing, relaxing weekend.

7. Practice the Silence for three to four hours a day. Unplug the phone, e-mail, radio, and television. Listen to Synergy and or Vibrational Medicine Music by Ivy. This sound is permitted while in the silence. Just go deep within yourself and see what your soul has to say.

8. Make the Master Cleanser Lemonade Drink. The Master cleanser is the most famous cleansing diet on the market these days. The Primary objective of the "Lemonade Diet" is to dissolve and eliminate toxins and mucus congestion which has formulated in the body over a long period of time. This is a great weekend detoxification that is very easy and inexpensive.

• Squeeze 1 cup of lemon or lime juice into glass

measuring cup. (real fresh organic lemons or limes)

- Pour 3 Tbsp genuine maple syrup into measuring cup. (be sure that it is organic)

- Blend a pinch of cayenne pepper or (red pepper), into the measuring cup.

- Pour ingredients into one gallon of spring water or distilled water. Shake and refrigerate.

- Drink nothing but this drink all weekend, until 6pm on Sunday.

Note: Be mindful to gradually return to solid food. Start with soup and steamed vegetables for example.

The maple syrup has minerals and vitamins that are very healthy for the system. If you are really up for a major cleansing, it is a good practice to use this formula for 10 days or more. Some have been successful at this detoxing cleanse for up to 40 days. This is a great practice for every change of the season. It also is a great source for relieving mental congestion. The Master Cleansing Diet was founded by Mr. Stanley Burroughs to bring us hope, knowledge and the truth.

5. Prepare yourself for a visualization exercise…Ideally; your visualization session should last for 20 minutes. You can begin with 10 minutes until you reach 20. Light an

aroma candle to diffuse your room with healing essential oils and play soft vibration healing music on the Serenity CD by Ivy. Before you begin, take a few minutes to relax yourself both physically and mentally, make sure you are sitting comfortably, and then focus your mind. There will be two visualization sessions a day for the entire weekend, this includes Friday evening. The cumulative effect of this ritual is most beneficial. By the fifth session on Sunday evening you should find your mind is becoming much clearer and calmer. When the session is finished, do not jump up immediately. Remain seated for a few minutes, breathing slowly, and try to retain the tranquility for the rest of the evening.

Mental Visualization Exercise

Close your eyes and picture a calming and relaxing place or a beautiful object, real or imagined that you see solely with your mind's eye. Observe this in the greatest detail, focusing on it completely. Gently refocus your attention on a place of tranquility, such as a deserted beach with crystal clear water, or floating in a bed of hibiscus flowers with a strong Caribbean aroma of the sea. Allow this visualization to take you on a journey of peace and joy. Play healing music in the background while conducting this mental visualization. Be sure that you are in a comfortable place and position for this exercise. You can use this time to work mentally on your life dreams. See the details of your hearts desires in their fullest manifestation in your visualization. Use this time to formulate how you will get the details accomplished and pay attention to the fine details of every step that it will take for you to realize your heart's desire. Be mindful not to think too hard on this visualization, allow the images to appear and watch them in your minds' eye as if you were watching a movie screen of your life. This visualization exercise is a lot of fun, and very powerful to practice. What you can conceive in your mind, can be realized in your life experience much faster than having no vision at all. Now that you can visualize your heart's deepest desires, you have become a visionary...so fly!

Create Healing Baths for the Weekend

1. Take an aroma bath and make a mud mask with a health drink.

2. Blend sea salt and baking soda together with lavender, jasmine and a dash of peppermint.

3. Take an Epsom Salt hot bath with seven pounds of salt. (do not use if you have high blood pressure)

4. Take a salt body scrub bath. This is a luxury treatment found in many health spas around

the world. It is guaranteed to start your day with a boost of energy. A salt body scrub has a number of beneficial effects, all of them stimulating to the system.

a. It clears the pores; sloughs away dead skin cells, so your skin is fresher and smoother.

b. It also stimulates the circulation and the elimination of toxins through the lymphatic system.

c. It stimulates cell renewal.

d. It will make your skin tingle and glow with vital energy.

PREPARING THE BODY SALT SCRUB

There are many exfoliates on the market, yet one of the best is simple sea or Dead Sea salt. You should use rock salt in flakes rather than a fine salt (except on the face). You can apply it directly to your body in handfuls, but it is easier to work with if you mix it into a paste with olive or sesame oil. This has the added advantage of nourishing the skin at the same time. You will need a handful of coarse rock salt and two tablespoons of olive oil or sesame oil. You can also experiment with **Afrikan Shea Butter**. If you would like an aroma feeling, add one to two drops of rose or lavender oil. Mix all of the ingredients together in a bowl and take this with you into the bathroom. Make sure that the bathroom is warm and that you have plenty of warm towels and a terry cloth bath robe nearby. Begin to rub the salts onto your body in an upward motion. Really get into the movement of your hands slowly and gently caressing your skin. Be careful not to scratch your skin by rubbing and chaffing the skin with the salt.

ENJOY YOUR JOURNEY INTO INNER PEACE

Where can I find GOD?

I am the light, the center of Inner Peace and Serenity

I am the shimmering light, reflecting in the cool waters of the earth from the Moonlight and the stars

I am the light, and I am in the light, flickering in the center of your candle burning in the midnight hour

I am the wind whispering in your ear while caressing your face gently with my assuring love

I am the light and love of the world, and you will find me wherever you are in the midst of your life's storm, gently and patiently *awaiting your attention to focus deep within the center of Serenity and Inner Peace, there is where you will find me*

Inner Peace, Serenity and the Light are the passageways into the presence of GOD

Keep your thoughts on God and you will surely maintain consistency in your Journey into Inner Peace

I am that I am I am that I am I am that I am.....

Amen

Namaste

And So It Is

AbSaHu RaKa

IF YOU HAVE ANY HOME SACRED RELAXATION IDEAS TO SHARE, SEND ME AN E-MAIL AND LOOK FOR IT ON MY WEBSITE AND FACEBOOK PAGE.

www.serenityhealingarts.com

E-mail- serenityliving31@aol.com@

Stay in the Light of Love

Resources for Creating Serenity & Inner Peace

Places to Go, People to See, and Things to Do

Serenity Healing Arts Wellness Education and Holistic Services,
Reverend Ivy .....Minister of Healing & Spiritual Living Coach
Transformational Tools for Empowering Your Life

"Come and rest for a while in a place where the mind-body & spirit find healing, purpose and inner peace."
Experience Intuitive Soul Therapy : A process for discovering your life purpose and opens the passageway to living out your life mission by re-patterning negative thought energy into positive thought energy. Releasing old thought patterns which have manifested into non-productive habitual ways. Use *Aroma Touch Therapy with doTERRA Essential Oils (www.mydoterra.com/serenityhealingarts)* in Meditation and the healing breath rituals, **Hypnotherapy** for releasing stress, communicating with the angels, releasing pain and post trauma conditions, **Reiki Healing** to calm the mind, body, spirit in preparation for the body and soul to communicate synergistic messages for growth and understanding, **Reflexology** for releasing stress, tension and dis-ease prevention, a blissful, profound experience of total relaxation and healing.
Experience the *Sound Vibronics Transformative Sonic Alignment-Full Body Meditation.* Create an instant

shift in consciousness, improve your focus, clear mental congestion, release stress and reach deep, deep levels of relaxation.

Healing Arts workshops and classes: Sound Vibronics™ ~ Sonic Meditation, Sensoriuim Sound Therapy, Ear Candling, Mindful Meditation, Serenity Living with Essential Oils, Learning to Play the Angelic Healing Harp, Study the Healing Attributes of Singing Crystal Bowls and Vibrational Medicine ~ Thought Shifting for Positive Attraction.

Inspirational Women Empowerment Program; Personal Healing Retreats, Spa Journey's, Inner Peace Sonic Meditations & Concerts, Travel with Rev. Ivy to exotic places for rest and rejuvenation Retreats.

Healing Temple of Light Ministries
Spiritual Marriage Ceremonies – Funerals -House Blessings – Marriage Counseling – Couples Counseling - Spiritual Healing Retreats –Spiritual Revivals
E-mail: ivyhylton@aol.com

Serenity Living Private Collection & Ivy's Meditation Music
***On-Line Boutique*.....** By Rev. Ivy
Purchase Singing Crystal Bowls, Om Tuning Forks. Meditation Ting Shaw Bells, Energy Chimes, Ivy's Meditation & Synergy Music on Compact Disc, Self Help and Spiritual Healing Books, Water Fountains, Tea Therapy, Exotic Resins, Aromatherapy , (Young Living Oils), Beeswax Candles, Relax Comfort Wear, Sound Vibronics Brain Wave Sonic Stress Reduction CD's, featuring Ivy's Relax Comfort Wear Collection.

301. 395.0460
Serenityliving31@aol.com
www.serenityhealingarts.com
www.thewellnesssalon.com
www.heavenhouseretreat.com
www.mydoterra.com/serenityhealingarts

Miracle Health and Chiropractic Center
Dr. Alison F. Henderson, Chiropractor
Do TERRA Oils - Full Body Health Scans - Chiropractic Services - Iridology - Car Accidents -Aqua Chi Foot Detox - The Reconnection
Featuring the Famous HCG Diet – Lose 30 lbs in 30 days $99.00
A compassionate healer, dedicated to the well-being of all people whose lives come into her space for healing. Take the time to release the pain and replace it with your life back to where it began before the pain. Hands on massage, essential oil and heat treatment, iridology, hydro therapy, water chi machine treatments, herbal supplements and meditation music by Ivy Hylton.
Washington, D.C. – Maryland – Virginia
202.550.0347 Office
aahdiva@yahoo.com

Simplexity Consulting Firm
Rev. Mutima Imani
Founder/CEO
Based in Oakland California, Rev. Mutima travels around the world creating positive solutions and effective training programs for organizations, global crisis intervention and trauma response services. She designs spiritual healing retreats empowering women and girls to work together

for the betterment of their families, churches and communities. A powerful inspiration for world healing, she designs rites of passage programs as the Queen Reverend Mutima Imani, offering Universal prayers for healing ourselves, children, families and leaders of the world. A sensitive and powerful spiritual healer, offering conscious manifestation readings, executive life coaching services, massage therapy and plenary speaker for blessing programs, conferences, and special events.
(Spiritual Healing, Massage Therapy, Conscious Transformation Consultations)
www.mutimaimani.com
510.205.4069

Kathy English Holt, HypnoMassage Therapist
New Therapy Promises Successful Results
HypnoMassage Therapy – Aromatherapy – Steam Treatments – Products- Silent Retreats on the Beach.
Nationally Certified in Therapeutic Massage & Body Work
Teacher & Educator gifted with the talents of creative and healing arts.
Transpersonal Hypno Therapist – Escape to Kathy's Massage Spa and discover your new reality......
HypnoMassage results into a valuable tool for self review, observation and personal understanding.
Call Kathy 202.986.1837

INTERNAL FOCUS
Ngozie Hall, Hydro Therapist
Colon Hydrotherapy is an internal washing of the colon using a high tech machine designed to cleanse toxic waste from the colon. This is a gentle and safe

procedure conducted by trained certified professionals. Colon Hydrotherapy is a gentle infusion of warm filtered water, which is circulated throughout the large intestine, dissolving fecal matter and other waste products from the colon. The waste material is removed without unpleasant odors or major discomfort. Ngozie also offers massage therapy, Reiki and herbal counseling services.
2913 Georgia Avenue N.W.
Washington, D.C.
202.232.3706

Zuri Nia, MSS, Touchologist
Healing Touch, ETC.
"A Safe Space to Connect with Your Authentic Self" Zuri
Shiatsu Deep Tissue/Reiki Master/ Ear Candling/ Clutter Buster Services/Chakra Movement Meditation/Ageless yoga
"The power of touch is to be touched" A Center for Soul Expression
301.681.0609
Silver Spring, Maryland
healervibe@yahoo.com
www.zuri@wellnesswithnia.com

Nata'ska Hassan Hummingbird
Aka WAPAJEA – "Walks on Water"
Storyteller-Vocalist-Songwriter-Urban Bush Woman-Keeper of the land-Spiritual Healer
(Mountain Eagle Place) – Spiritual Healing Center – "Where Traditional Lives On"
In loving memory of Mountain Eagle Woman, we love you deeply Mommi.

434.848.4315
mteagleplace@gmail.com
www.mountaineagleplace.com

Victoria Paytonwebber "The Harpist"
Electric & Acoustic Harps and Vocals
When the Ordinary Just Won't Do
DC Federation of Musicians Local 161-710
Experience ....Victoria the Harpist's meditation music, music for weddings, studio recordings and keyboard lessons.
Experience Victoria's Healing Music
301.899.8689

"Yasmeen" Betty Williams
Independent Entertainment Professional
Healing the World in Gospel Song
Summer Records Newly posted videos
Couldn't Hear Nobody Pray
60 Million
Believe it
They are the Number
Follow Yasmeen Summer Music on
www.YouTube.com

The Ark of Self-Healing & Self H.E.L.P.
"Conscious Living through Living Consciously"
Stepping Up Out of the Dark Ages of Disease Care & Nutricide
Improve lymphatic health, increase cardiovascular flow of life, increase energy, enhance emotional mood, prevent disease and illness.
Dr. Karen Davis-Foulks

Lymphologist, Nutri-Energetics Practitioner & Life Extension Nutritionalist
202.248.7749
www.4celllife.com

Academy for Ideal Education
Community Based Family-Centered Education
Paulette Jones-Imaan
Director & Founder
The Academy for Ideal Education is a coed private school in Washington DC. A non sectarian holistic home learning environment, serving grades PK-12. Children learn meditation and
1501 Gallatin Street, NW
Washington, DC 20011
202.726.0313
www.idealschooldc.org

Dove Center, Dove Healing Arts
Dr. Atiba Vheir, Ph.D., D.D.
Integrative Holistic Wellness Programs
Lectures, seminars, training, retreats, full rites of passage programs for adults.
Classes in Transpersonal Studies and Transpersonal Psychology
202.265.1348
AtibaVheir@aol.com

Manifest Innertainment, LLC
Manifest Ra, Certified Qigong Instructor
Life Balancing Expert – Qigong classes and monthly ULM events
Founder of Heal Humanity and the Universal Love Movement (ULM)

Twitter.com/manifestRa123
202.746.4537

Inner Visions Worldwide
Iyanla Vanzant
Best Selling Author, Spiritual Life Teacher, Television and Radio Personality
Institute for Spiritual Development
"We offer ourselves in the Service of God's people by providing an arena for spiritual awakening and strengthening"
Spiritual Life Coaching
Workshops-Holistic Services-Ministerial Ordination
301.419.8085
www.innervisionsworldwide.com

Emma Mae Gallery
The Rev. Sandra Butler-Truesdale
Proprietor
Specializing in the Historical Preservation and Exhibition of Rhythm, Blues, Jazz and Gospel
Featuring the Heavens Art Café
Customized Framing and Community Empowerment
202.246.6300
www.emmamaegallery.com

The Ministries of
The Rev. Sandra Butler-Truesdale, Inc.
Weddings, Funerals, Ordinations, Services, Senior Programs, Promoting the Healing & Performing Arts
Sandra2001@verizon.net
202.246.6300

The Energy Institute of the Healing Arts, Inc.
Herbal Therapy, Therapeutic Services, Nutritional Therapy, Hypnotherapy-Certification Classes
Rev. Dr. Akmal
Dedicated to promoting wellness and optimal health through therapeutic healing modalities and programs. Through the use of Traditional Chinese Healing Arts, Oi Gong Healing, Breath work and rebirthing.
12911 Woodmore Road
Mitchellville, MD 20721
310.249.2445
www.healen.net

Rev. Denise Hylton
Sound Shama
Offering indigenous Sound Healing, Sonic Massage and Harmonic Medicine through Integrative Therapy, Workshops, Seminars and Sedna Gong Meditations.
Community education programs and professional educational seminars. Supporting family wellness.
570.369.4092
revdenise@soundshama.com
www.soundshama.com

Giving Reiki Touch
Reiki for Everything
Faye Drummond/Joyce L. Graham
"You must get to know the **Reiki** sisters.......In the presence of their space, Miracles Happen".
Classes, Healing Services, Reiki Energy Shares, Trips around the world visiting ancient healing vortexes, and meeting healers from all traditions.

Faye Drummond, M.A, M. P.H.

Karuna Reiki Master Teacher
301.229.2485
Faye is my personal Reiki Healing Practitioner, and I know that Miracles Happen for me when I am in her Healing Studio in Bethesda Maryland. Schedule your appointment today.

Joyce L. Graham, M.H.S.

Karuna Reiki Master Teacher
Joyce is a master planner, powerful healer and spiritual intuitive ready to embrace you in the space of healing energy in Olney Maryland.. Schedule your appointment today
301.774.6109
www.givingreikitouch.com

ENOMIS Oasis Spa / Spiritual Oasis Foundation

"You Deserve to be Pampered"
Rev. Viviana Brown, LMT
Massage Therapist, Reiki Master, Board Certified Colon Hydrotherapist, Hot Stone Aromatherapy Massage and more.
10101 Georgia Avenue
Silver Spring, Maryland 20902
301.585.6479
Spiritualoasis1@aol.com
www.enomisoasis.com

Sasheps Ari-a,lle

Ammen M. Khitasa
Therapeutics and Holistic Wellness
Relaxation and Stress Relief- Mobile on-site Services
Table or Seated Massage
240.398.4307

Words to Live By
Coaching, Workshops & Products Providing Life Changing Results- "Oh yes it does"
Denise J. Hart
The Motivation Mama!
202.321.0779
www.motivationmama.com (blog)

Sisterspace and Books
A Global Space for Global Citizens
"Walk by Faith and not by Sight"
Owned by Sister Fay Williams
Greetings Sisters and Brothers, Friends and Customers, Philanthropists and Investors,
Back in the day, **Georgia Avenue** was the location for black-owned businesses. **Sisterspace and Books** is a part of that tradition and we need you to support us, if we are to be around and able to do our work. We are happy to be back to serve the community – and we need your continued support.
3717 Georgia Avenue, NW
Washington DC, 20010
202.829.0306
www.sisterspacedc.com

Positive Energy Works
Iyo Handy-Kendi, CTBF,CSM, CEO
Positive Energy Breath Coach
Relearn how to BREATHE
FOR BETTER LIFE< HEALTH & WORK™
Power of the Breath Tour
Breath Work, workshops, life coaching, diversity training, wellness events.

Become a certified Breathologist- "The Cleansing Breath"
202.667.2577
www.BreathePositive.com

Beyond Empowerment
Charlene Springer ~ Radio Talk Show Host
Charlene shares of herself by hosting her own radio show entitled "Beyond Empowerment" on WSTX AM 970. The show focuses on exploring new ideas, sharing spirituality, and creating new solutions for empowering women of our community.
WSTX AM970
Tuesday Mornings
10am - 12noon
Listen in online
www.wstxam.com

Alda E. Anduze
PHOTOGRAPHY FOR ALL OCCAISIONS
A St. Croix native, Alda has over twenty years experience as a professional photographer both around the islands and stateside. Alda is passionate in everything she does, exuding positivity that is so infectious that her presence uplifts the spirits of everyone around her. When not behind the camera, Alda (highest level female blackbelt in the Caribbean) teaches martial arts at her Sunsu Dojo karate studio and spends time with the families of six grown sons. On Sundays she can be seen decked out in leathers riding her Harley with the St. Croix Rain Riders.
340.718.1274
340.513.3670
www.aldaanduze.com

Sunsu Dojo
Sansei Isshinryo Karate – Do
"Gentleness can only be expected from the strong"
Karate is a martial art that was perfected in Okinawa after many centuries in China. It is based upon both mental and physical discipline. It is considered to be one of the finest forms of exercise. Karate is not merely an excellent physical exercise for self-defense. The complete control required for the mastery of physical movements, the efforts and discipline required in the search for the ultimate mastery of the art, lies in the foundation and development of good citizenship and the ultimate in self confidence. With these qualities, Karate can become the ultimate perfection of human character.
235 La Grand Princess
St. Croix, USVI 00820
340.718.1274

Ayana's Amazing Belly Fat Reducer
Get rid of belly fat with exotic herbs, coupled with a handmade clay solution. It is not a weight loss wrap…. however; you lose 1 to 4 inches with lymphatic flushing system.
Make your appointment now
Baltimore Maryland
410.466.5047

The Performing Arts Training Studio
Denise J. Hart, Owner, Master Instructor, Mind Set Coach
The Studio is under the direction of award winning Actress, Director Playwright, and Master Instructor Denise J. Hart, a native Omahan with over 25 years

experience in the Performing Arts. She is a tenured Associate Professor of theatre at Howard University and a Creativity Coach. Through performing with Wolly Mammoth Theatre with Harold Shalwitz, H Street Playhouse with Jeremy Skidmore, Arena Stage, African Continuum Theatre and in the recurring role of "Miss Anna" on HBO's The WIRE, as well as leading a host of professional workshops and classes around the country, Denise has gained a depth of professional experience that definitively shapes her perspective on training both the novice and professional. Featuring, the "Mind Spa" and Motivational MaMa Mind Set Coaching Services.

6925 Willow Street NW
1st Fl
(between N Aspen St & N Sandy Spring Rd)
Washington, DC 20012
Neighborhood: Takoma
(202) 321-0779
www.tctwstudio.com

Massage Personified
"Touch the gift to life"
By Jada
Certified Massage Therapist
By appointment only
202.387.6997

Mountain Mystic Trading Company
Unique Gifts and Tools for an Evolving Age
215 B South Street
Front Royal, VA 22630
540.635.6318
www.mountainmystic.com

The Natural Path to Wellness Foundation, Inc.
Providing naturopathic and spiritual healing services, African mission work, workshops, and retreats
Dr. Akua N. Zenzele/ President/Co-Founder
6101 Parkway Drive
Baltimore, MD 21212
www.naturalpathtowellness.org

Prime Time Sister Circle
The Gaston & Porter Health Improvement Center
Marilyn Hughes Gaston, M.D. – Former Assistant General of the United States Public Health Service
Gayle K. Porter, Psy.D, - Principle Research Analyst and Senior Mental Health Advisor for the American Institute for Research.
Authors of The African American Woman's Complete Guide to Midlife Health and Wellness
Vision: All Women, especially African American women, will choose and live a life designed to maximize their emotional and physical health.
Mission: To revolutionize the way women think, feel and act about prioritizing their physical and emotional health & wellness.
www.gastonandporter.org

Serenity Wellness
Cheryl J. Jackson, CMSR, CAPPM
President/CEO
Don't Just Live, Live Healthy
Wellness International Network (WIN)
703.403.7392
www.serenity-wellness.com

Avalaura's Healing Center
Where Genuine Healing Happens Naturally
Avalaura G. Beharry, MSW,LGSW
Holistic Healer, Counselor & Teacher
By appointment only
301.675.8723
www.avalaura.com

Neshama Soulworks Studio
Transforming life with art and soul
Jennifer Judelson, LCSW
Psychotherapist, Artist, Educator
703.256.0485
www.soulworksstudio.com

Black Women's Health Imperative
1726 M. Street, NW
Suite 300
Washington, DC 20036
202.548.4000
www.BlackWomensHealth.ORG

Elise Braithwaite, MS, LMT, RYT
National Certified and Licensed Massage Therapist
Swedish, Deep Tissue, Pregnancy Massage
Certified Yoga Teacher
Reiki Master
202.581.0770

After the Trauma
Helping Survivors of Domestic Violence Re-Establish
Their Lives
Mildred D. Muhammad
Executive Director
www.afterthetrauma.org

Tejase Bodyworks
Illuminating the goodness within
Therapeutic Massage/Yoga
Christina Page, LMT,RYT
504.535.6188
www.tejasebodyworks.abmp.com

REIKI & Master Alignment
Pam Sanders, RN
Energy Healing
304.258.0256

Reflexology
Martha J. Sikes
Certified Refelxologist
Awakening Health Center
51 Independence Street
Berkeley Springs, WV 25411
304.258.6678
www.awakeninghealthcenter.com

Allowing The Light
Shamanic Healings
Beatrice Pouligny
202.436.6125
allowingthelight@gmail.com

MASSAGE
Relaxing…Soothing…Rejuvenating
Evelyn Garcia
Massage Therapist/Neuromuscular Therapy
By appointment only
304.258.9069

Gentle Yoga Classes
Joyce Morningstar Barron, RYT
Star Eagle Studio
1437 Pious Ridge Rd.
Berkeley Springs, WV 25411
Ongoing Classes Stretching & Basic Breathing Practices
– Relieve Stress…love your body
304.258.6247
joycemorningstar@peoplepc.com

StarEagle Studio
A Center for the Living Arts
Joyce Morningstar Barron
Lee Hearteagle Barron
Home of the Amethyst Signing Crystal Bowl
Hand Made Jewelry, Iris Gardens, Yoga, Handmade
Herbal Soaps
1437 Pious Ridge Road
Berkeley Springs, WV 25411
304.258.6247
www.stareaglestudio.com

Ascension Fashion Group
Leighel Desiree, Designer/CEO
www.leigheldesiree.com
www.acensionfashionmagazine.com

Ancient Healing Through Beauty Culture
Worn-Again Naturalist
"Natural hair is your birthright..claim it, love, it, wear it
and discover yourself through it"
513.307.0017
info@wornagain.org
www.wornagain.org

~Spa. Nia~
Massage Therapy with a Purpose
Theresa Robinson, LMT
Bt appointment only
202.526.7244

Hadiah's Holistic Haven, L.L.C
Meditation Yoga Awareness
Balancing Energy Centers.
202.829.6863
www.hadiaha.holistichaven.com

Healing Hands Massage Institute and In-Home Spa Services
J'Huti TaSeti
Infra red treatments, hot massage stones, foot massage and body transformation alignment treatments-release pain from tight muscles, soreness, arthritis.
Founder, Workshop Facilitator
202.413.2047

Fountains of Life
Wellness Center and Detoxification Spa
Release * Replenish * Relax
Offering Colon Hydrotherapy, Aqua Chi Foot Baths, Ear Candling, Oxygen Sauna Therapy, Hot Aroma Steam Treatments, Bio Active Frequency Therapy and more…..
Contact the Spa for your treatment today
www.fountainsoflife.net
e-mail at Fountainsoflifespa@gmail.com
202.332.3100

Rainbow of Life
Wellness Center and Detox
Total Detox Center:
Colon HydroTherapy
Hyperbaric Oxygen Chamber
Aroma Steam Therapy
Foot Baths
Oral Chelations
Liver Flushes
Contact: 480.733.4638
www.rainbowoflifeAZ.net
Email: mickcolon@aol.com

Prevagen
Brain Cell Protection
Healthier Brain – Sharper Mind – Clearer Thinking
www.prevagen.com www.quincybioscience.com
1.888.818.MIND(6463)

Natural Rhythms
Health & Wellness , Dr. Tilli Williams, Wellness
Physician
202. 547.WELL (9355)
Washington, D.C.
www.drtilli.com

Ange Anglade Fitness
Optimum health inside and out Decide. Commit.
Succeed.
Online Fitness Coaching Services
BeFit in Mind, Body and Soul using Beachbody Home
Fitness videos and programs to help transform your body.
301.404.6045
www.angeangladefitness.com

Justice in Health Care
Ratrini H. Nyasumah, R.N.
Reflexology, Polarity Therapy, Somatic Touch
Rescuing the Inner Child
e-mail: chakra4@earthlink.net
202.575.4325

Harmony 4 U
Juanita Kae Eldridge
Harmony Mentor
444Harmony@Gmail.com
202.340.1507

Terry Victor, D.D.S.
Holistic/Biological Dentistry
A Dentist for your Mind. Body & Spirit…Not just your teeth!!
301.326.5365
Silver Spring, Maryland
Tvictor_dds@hotmail.com

Natural, Integrative, Complimentary Services
Dr. G.N. Douglas-Harper, N.C.N.M.
202.544.4478
Washington, D.C.

Sacred Healing Herbal Body Wrap
DeAnna DeWitt
Stress free, Healthy and Alive
Transition to a healthier you
Detox, Lose inches, and reduce cellulite, 100% safe, firm, tone and condition the skin.
Certified Body Wrap Professional
Beltsville, Maryland
240.882.3578

Organic Soul Chef
Raw and Living Food Preparation
Madea A. Gueye
Living food preparation classes, demonstration and food preparation for health and wealth. Holistic Nutrition and natural organic food and products. Specializing in ION Water.
347.247.5208
www.organicsoulchef.com
http://madeaebony.yourbodyiswater.com   Distributor# 6148078

ALOS
Art Jewelry – silver and precious stones
202.294.9714
www.alos-artjewelry.com

ZURESH FACE
Hair and body products to enhance your natural beauty
FACIAL-BODY-HAIR CARE - MAKE UP
Specializing in skin disorders (eczema, psoriasis, dermatitis, lupus, cancer etc)
Mia Lee: 202.412.2974
P.O. Box 539
Bladensburg, MD 20710
www.zuresh.com
info@zuresh.com

ICONIC LEE
The Hottest Handcrafted Pillows, Purses & Accessories on the PLANET!
Steven Lee
202.412.2973
info@iconiclee.com
www.iconiclee.com

Loving Care Nature Center
Raw Foods, Child Care, Meditation, all natural health products
P.O. Box 2006, Montgomery Village, Maryland 20886-2006
301.417.0955
lovingcare@erols.com

Zho Lin Yang, O.M.D. Clinic
Acupuncture & Herbal Medicine
202.232.0549

Circle of Light
We are a Journey to Wellness
Holistic Health Practices & Interfaith Ministry Services
301.537.6091
www.circleoflightim.com to see the calendar of events

Journey African American Outdoor Sports Association
Hiking, road-cycling, kayaking, car-camping, rock climbing, backpacking. Horse-back-riding and more
410.448.9048
www.journeyoutdoors.com

Hixon Holistic Life Center
Health and Wellness Lecture Series, Self-Improvement Classes, Optimal Health Radio Show 88.9 F.M.
Eleanor Hixon M.D.
410.788.4477
www.hixonholisticlife.com

Rituals: A Spa Wellness System
Denise Mclane-Davison, MSW,CEO

The Process of Rituals Self-Care Products
Helping to unify mind, Body, Spirit for Overall Well-Being
404.610.7391
Snellville, Georgia
ritualsspa@hotmail.com

Girlfriends Beauty Boutique & Creative Hair & Nail Designs

Hair, Nails, Products, Jewelry, Clothing
202.526.2057
Washington, D.C.

IDA's IDEA

Designers Boutique… (clothing for serenity living)
"Come by and Be IDALyzed"
931 7th Street, N.W.
Washington, D.C. 20001
(one block from the convention center)
202.408.7904
Idasidea1@aol.com

BROWN BAG ANGELS

International Angels designed from brown paper bags
Robyn Outerbridge
www.brownbagangels.com

Nisey's Boutique

Everything Unique for Serenity Living…join the MONEY in your pocket for referrals program (the Community Favorite)
4007 34th Street
Mt Rainier, MD 20712
301.277.7977
www.niseysboutique.com

Slam Your Stress
Creative Expression Workshop
Ty Gray-EL, CSMT. Slamthologist
202.528.8868
www.slamyourstress.com

Lisa M. Green, A.A.L.L. Limited
Harmonious Cultural Art Expressions
Powerful, Breath Taking, A Must to Have of Your Own
for Serenity Living
240.350.6364
www.aall-artonline.com (a must to see!)

CELEBRATE!
Floral Designs & Event Management
Pat Carpenter
703.980.2143
www.celebrateevents.net

BY ANY GREENS NECESSARY
Tracye McQuirter, M.P.H.
Nutritionist & Author
202.615.5496
www.byanygreensnecessary.com

Blue Nile Botanicals
Over 300 bulk herbs & spices
A community favorite
Duku & Kweku, African Herbmen
202.232.3535
Washington, D.C.
www.bluenilebotanicals.com

PORTALS
A New Age Shoppe
Unique Products, Classes & Events
Healing Services, books and healing instruments
304.258.5200
Berkley Springs, West Virginia
www.PORTALSOFBERKELEYSPRINGS.COM

"Special T" Dolls & Designs
From the Heart & Soul
Tamara J. Thomas
Artist & Designer
Dolls with spirit, serenity, sass & class
P.O. Box 131
Bladensburg, MD 20710
301.779.5664
SpecialTDollArt@yahoo.com
Peace, blessings and love

Young Living Essential Oils
Visit this web-site and purchase essential oil products. You may also call the 800 number and speak with a trained sales representative to help you make your selections.
1.800.371.2928
Your products will come directly to your door.
www.youngliving.com

GAIAM Living
The essence of mind-body health products for *Serenity Living*. Shop for thousands of products online; anytime. Read informative articles, access product information.
1.800. 254.8464
www.gaiam.com

Pacific Spirit
Whole Life Products
Products for creating a wellness lifestyle.
1.800.634.9057
Call for a new catalogue to be mailed to your home

ADACI
Ancestor Altars
Constructed for all events and occasions; specifically created to pay tribute to your ancestors and the African deities.
African Diaspora Ancestral Commemoration Institute
202.558.2187
301.292.6822 ~ 443.570.5667
WWW.ADACI.NET

DAR ES SALAAM
(House of Peace)
Book/Health Center
Hampton Mall
9185 Central Ave.
Capitol Heights, MD 20743
301.350.3388
BrotherHodari@gmail.com
www.DESBOOKS.vpweb.com

The Master Cleanser, Enhance Healing with the Vita-Flex Video
Relax-A-Roller (Promoting circulation and relieving tension)
P.O. Box 30044 3346
Reno, NV 89520-3044

Herbal Healer Academy, Inc.
Natural Medicine Supply Catalog
Leader in Effective, Alternative, Natural Medicine and Education
870.269.4177
Call to get on the mailing list and request a catalog
www.herbalhealer.com

Dudley Products
Changing Lives by Changing Faces
Skin Care, Glamour, Spa Products, Career
1.800.334.4150
www.dudleycosmetics.com

Scrip Massage and Spa Supply
Products for creating *Serenity Living*, spa treatments, massage tools, books, videos, music, software, exercise, rehabilitation, charts, posters. Resources for creating a Spa in your Home.
1.800. 747.3488 call for catalog
www.scripmassage.com
info@scripmassage.com

POTTERY BARN
Furniture for **Serenity Living**, workspaces, home accessories, great decoration ideas, indoor and outdoor living.
1.800 .922.5507
24- Hours, call for catalog
www.potterybarn.com

The Heritage- A legacy for Life
Personal Care Products to Enhance Your Health & Well-Being

Complete supplier of Edgar Cayce Products
Located in Virginia Beach, Virginia
1. 800.862.2923 (call for catalogue)

Agape Jewelry Designs Inspired by God
Designed by Cynthia
202.829.7843
Washington, D.C.

Paradise Fabrics and Fashion Designers
Wholesale * Retail * Fabric from Around the World
Abdusemed Ibrahim
301.568.3938
Suitland, Maryland

NEW LIFE SYSTEMS
Spa and Salon Solutions to create a Spa in your Home.
Skin care products, stone therapy, masks, paraffin
products. hydrotherapy, ear candling and more.
1.800.852.3082 (call for catalog)
www.newlifesystems.com
Email: infor@newliesystems.co

Living Earth Crafts
Bodywork Accessories
Massage tables, shiatsu tables, massage chairs, books,
massage tables flannel sheet and blankets, hand massage
products, anatomy charts and more.
1.800. 358.8292
Call for a catalog

Sienna Interiors, LLC/Sienna At Home
5152 Buffalo Speedway, Houston TX 77005 (713) 665-
5534
www.sienna_at_home.com

Home Spa Essentials
Pearlessence® 2008
Aroma Diffusers- air & water Therapy – spa essentials
Featuring (spa mist diffusers, spa lights and stone water fountains
26201 Richmond Road Cleveland Oh 44146
216.464.3300 800.648.5153
www.pearlessence.com

Lowe's Home Improvement Stores *(Located all over the United States)*
Create a *Serenity Living* environment with colorful paints, wall paper, accessories etc.
Look for serenity idea magazines:
1. ARCHITECTURAL   DIGEST   – International Magazine of Interior Design
2. BATHROOM TRENDS – Where ideas take shape
3. Ideas for Great HOME LIGHTING – Stylish and Practical Lighting Options for indoors and Out
4. Better Homes and Gardens WINDOW TREATMENTS – Defining moods, strategy, and style.
5. Decorating with Paint & Color
6. Explore the lighting section for special lighting treatments. Be creative, bold and innovative with your ideas.

Ivy's Favorite Serenity Living Retreats and Spas

AYANA~ Natural Body Care and Healing
Enhancing Your Spirit and Well-Being
Private Spa & Wellness Resource
410.466.5047
Ayanascents@comcast.net
Baltimore Maryland
By referral or invitation
Massage and More ……..Customized Handmade aromatherapy blends and skin products-Toxin Awareness and Cleanse-Total Health Spa Body Treatment-Life Coaching- Multi Energy Spa Bed
www.Ayanascents.com

Medissage Retreat Center
Sacred Spaces for
Love ~Service ~Surrender
Centers for Health, Growth and Transformation
1117 Black Creek Church Road
Mount Croghan, South Carolina 29727
843.658.7063 843.658.7062 – fax 843.658.7065
www.medissage.org
info@medissage.org

Per Ankh Institute , Inc.
NswtMwtAst Dr. ChenziRa Davis Kahina aka Dr. Chen
NTR Therapist & Managing Director of Per Ankh Institute
Project Director of NUWOMANRising LIVE UP!

Author, Wellness Educator, Queen Poetess, Spiritual Leader, Community Activist.

Is an educational, cultural, artistic, holistic wellness & non-governmental organization & spiritual retreat center. At Per Ankh, we remain khamitted & livicated to the principles of Maat and Djhty as they are found within the Great Book of Nature & Life as Sesheta in Smai Tawi.

We are positively khamitted to integrating ancient & contemporary living science techniques for improving the lives of women, men & children for more balanced self-liberation & organized life ethics that nurture health, wellness, family & communitarian prosperity!

**Maat-Truth, justice, order, reciprocity, harmony, balance ~ Djhty-Divine Intelligence, thought & wisdom ~ Sesheta-Kosmik Memory Bank with NTRAA (Kreator Principles).

1.888.614.5554
1-340-244-2524 Voice1
1-888-614-5554 Fax/Msg
1-305-407-2654 Voice2/Msg
P.O. Box 607
Kingshill, St Croix VI 00851-0607
www.perankhu.org perankh@gmail.com
www.nuwomanrising.org nuwomanrising@gmail.com

PerAnkhLIVE!

Multiple weekly broadcasts on holistic living, health awareness, women's affairs, sustainable development, nationbuilding and healing for A Nu Humanity! Supports PerAnkh Khamniversity mission vision of Culture, Healing, Arts, Technology and Spirituality for Life, Inspiration, Freedom and Education=CHATS4LIFE!

www.blogtalkradio.com/perankhlive
www.innerlightradio.com
www.harambeeradio.com

Beulah African Methodist Episcopal Zion Church
Pastor, Rev. Richard Austin, Esquire
First Lady, Sister Nolly Austin
Sunday School: Sunday 9:30am
Church Services: Sunday 10:30am
Bible Study: Wednesday Nights 7:pm
For more information, call 340.778.8050
St Croix, Virgin Islands

Charlene Springer
Massage Aesthetician, Healer, Community Activist, Healing Light of Love
St. Croix Plastic Surgery & MEDISPA
Belief in higher light, higher consciousness and higher vibration. We are spiritual Beings having a human experience.

Charlene is the most recent addition to the St Croix Plastic Surgery family. She serves as an independent Aesthetician and offers a full range of integrated Spa Serivces. Her expertise includes Vodder Certification in Manual Lymphatic Drainage Therapy, a healing modality that is excellent for peri-operative swelling and musculoskeletal injuries. She is also an accomplished make-up artist. Charlene is well known in the St. Croix community, not only for excellence in her field, but also as an advocate for women's issues. (Offering a full range of integrated spa services)

12 Beeston Hill
Christiansted St. Croix, U.S.V.I. 00820
340.719.2777

Mountain Eagle Place Spiritual Healing Center
"Great Spirit We Come Humbly As We Know How"
Healing on the Land Where Tradition Lives On
Lover Weekend Getaways – Family Bonding – Workshops
and Classes – Healing Work – Connection with Great
Spirit – Silent Retreats – Youth Retreats
434.848.4315
www.mountaineagleplace.com
Lawrenceville Virginia

Massage Personified
By Jada
Holistic Massage Therapy for Seniors
202.387.6997

Salon del sol
Salon and Spa
804.323.9767
www.salondelsoandspa.com
Richmond, Midlothian, and Roanoke Virginia

The Spa at the CHESAPEAKE BEACH
Resort & Full Service Spa
4165 Mears Avenue
Chesapeake Beach, MD 20732
410.257.4464
www.chesapeakbeachresortspa.com

Serenity Space
Sylvia Small-Ehilen
Specializing in Massage Therapy for Fibromyalgia-The
Healing Power of Touch
muscle pain, chronic tension headaches
low back pain, daytime fatigue, Anxiety and depression,

insomnia and disturbed sleep pattern, restricted muscle function.
Swedish Relaxation-On-Site Chair Massage-Revitalizing Foot Soak and Massage
6323 Georgia Av. NW
Washington, D.C. 20011
Call My Sister Sylvia
202.297.0224

The Healing Tree
Detox and Wellness Spa
Foot Bath-Tui Na Back Rub, Thai Yoga Sacred Body Work
Steam Sauna, Massage and Birth Doula
Castor oil pack
Call Zatiti
Includes Raw Live Food or Vegan Lunch
240.277.7971
www.AHEALINGTREE.Com

KAMALAYA
KOH SAMUI
Thailand Wellness
Sanctuary and Holistic Spa Resort
Asia's Premier Destination Spa
At Kamalaya Koh Samui
Award Wining Wellness Sanctuary
Experience a life-enriching healthy holiday. Our wellness programs offer solutions for detox, yoga, stress and burnout, fitness and weight control
Call: +66.77.429.800
Email: info@kamalaya.com
www.kamalaya.com
"Paradise exists!"- Natlialie Pascale. February 2008

Bali Holistic Yoga Retreats
Massage, Yoga, Day Spa
Meditation, relaxation and rejuvenation
Call: +62.361.970.992
Email: answers@balispirit.com
www.balispirit.com

Anahata Natural Resort and Spa
Ubud, Bali
A natural spa retreat for mind~ Body ~ Spirit
Call: 62.361.978.991 or 978.992
www.anahata@resort.com

Bali Day Spa and Massage Center
Shangrila Spa – Ubud, Bali
#1 Spa in Ubud, Bali
Call: 031.919.2547
www.ubudmassage.com
Relax on the beach of Shangri-La after your spa treatments
and enjoy inner peace
www.bali-shangrila.com

SPA WORLD
Revitalizing Life
Specializing in Sauna Baths at high temperatures - Steam
Baths in enclosed stone dome-Poultice Rooms generating
radiant heat from natural earth elements such as hot red
clay, amethysts and more.
13830A 10 Braddock Road
Centerville, VA 20121
703.815.8959
www.spaworldusa.com

Parma Center for Health
Authentic Ayurvedic Massage Therapy
Hot stone, Deep Tissue, Anti-Aging and Hydrating Facials
Wonderful people and exclusive attention
8212 Old Courthouse Road
Vienna, Virginia 22182
703.506.8401
www.parmaspa.com

MASSAGE
Relaxing...Soothing...Rejuvenating
Evelyn Garcia
Massage Therapist/Neuromuscular Therapy
By appointment only
304.258.9069

Sand Castle on the Beach Resort
127 Estate Smithfield
Fredricksted, St. Croix
U.S. Virgin Islands, 00840
Tel: 340.772.1205
Sheryl & Simone, Proprietors
www.sandcastleonthebeach.com

ATASIA SPA
41 Congress Street
Berkeley Springs, WV 25411
1.877.258.7888
1.304.258.7888
www.atasiaspa.com

Berkeley Springs State Park
Spa and Bath House
Soak in the hot mineral springs and Swedish Massage
2 South Washington Street
Berkeley Springs, West Virginia 25411
304.258.2711
www.berkeleyspringssp.com

THE BATH HOUSE
All Treatments by Appointment
21 Fairfax Street
Berkeley Springs, WV 25411
304.258.9072 or 800.431.4698
Signature Skin Care Treatments-Spa Packages-Aroma
spa-Massage-Facials-Hot Stone Therapy-Pedicure
www.bathhouse.com

HOLLOWOOD
Retreat & Conference Center
A Ministry of Saint Luke Lutheran Church
Silver Spring, Maryland
7300 Banner Road
Comus, Maryland 20842-8010
1.301.831.8422
www.hollowood.org

STILLWATER SPA
The Journey of Renewal
Hyatt Regency Chesapeake Bay Resort & Spa
Cambridge, Maryland
410.901.1234 (Call to schedule a personal retreat massage
& SPA experience)
www.spahyatt.com

A.R.E. Health & Rejuvenation Center
Massage & Day Spa Services
Association for Research and Enlightenment, Inc.
Massage-Colonics- Hypnotherapy-Reflexology- Readings-
Wellness Assessments and much more
Edgar Casey Foundation
215 67th Street
Virginia Beach, Virginia 23451-2061
1.800.333.4499 757.437.7202
www.edgarcayce.org/hrc/

Agnihotra India
Perform Agnihotra. Heal the Atmosphere
www.Agnihotraindia.com

SECRETS OF NATURE
Health Foods, Café, Herbs, Teas, Essential Oils and
more
Coy G. Dunston
3923 South Capitol Street, SW
Washington, DC 20032
202.562.0041
www.Secretsofnature.com

VALLECITOS MOUNTAIN REFUGE
Fellowships for Spiritual Renewal and Meditation
Retreats
Carson National Forest
Taos, New Mexico
P.O. Box 3160
Taos, New Mexico, 87571
505.751.9613
www.valecitos.org

The Inn on Thistle Hill
Bed & Breakfast Wellness Center
In a Holistic Community
5541 Sperryville Pike
Boston, Virginia, 22713
540.987.9357
www.TheInnOnThistleHill.com

Capon Springs & Farms Retreat Center
Specializing in a place for Families & Friends to Gather
P.O. Box O
Capon Springs, West Virginia 26823
304.874.3695
www.26823.com

ESALEN Institute
Wellness Resort
55000 Highway One, Big SUR, CA 93920
831.667.3032
www.friends@esalen.org

The Woods
Resort & Conference Center
P.O. Box 5, Hedgesville, West Virginia 25427
1.800.248.2222
www.TheWoodsResort.com

Excel
Movement Studios
Pilates of Washington DC
3407 8th Street, NE,
Washington, DC 20017
202.269.3020
Empower Your Body....Empower Your Mind
www.excelpilates.com

Warm Springs Inn
P.O. Box 99, Warm Springs, Virginia 24484
Located directly across from the Warm Springs Healing
Mineral Bath Pool
540.839.5351

Peaceful River Campground
Rout 1 Box 90, Millboro, Virginia 24460
Located on the Cowpasture River
540.996.4256

SEASONS
A Center for Renewal
FETZER INSTITUTE
9292 West KL Avenue
Kalamazoo, Michigan 4900-9398
616.375.2000
www.fetzer.org

Unity Village Retreat Center
1901 Northwest Blue Parkway
Unity Village, MO 64065
816.251.3540
www.unityretreats.org

Personal Retreats at Roslyn
Episcopal Diocese of Virginia
8728 River Road
Richmond Virginia, 23229
804.288.6045 / 1.800.477.6296
www.roslyncenter.com

Nemacolin Woodlands Resort & Spa
1001 LaFayette Drive, Farmington, PA 15437
1.800.422.2736 or 724.329.8444
www.nemacolin.com

Destination Spa Group
Learn about the top 25 Destination Spas
Contact Spa Enthusiast for more details
A Newsletter for Healthy SPA Living From Your Day Spa
and Spa Finder
1.888.772.4363
www.desinationspa.com

American Spa Expo
Skincare*Cosmetics*Wellness
1.800.427.2420
www.americanspaexpo.com

Accessing Free Health Information from the Edgar Cayce website:
http://edgarcayce.org Library email: library@edgarcayce.org

- Diseases: http://www.edgarcayce.org/health/database/chdata/disease.html
- Contains overviews of specific disease conditions such as asthma, diabetes, hypertension, ulcers, etc.

- Therapies: http://www.edgarcayce.org/health/database/chdata/data/therapy.html
- Free online course in Meditation: http://www.are-cayce.org/ecreadings/Meditation/welcome.html

Sound Vibronics™
Healing Instruments

Singing Crystal Bowls

Tuning Fork

Singing Crystal Bowl and Body Tuner Starter Kit

1-10" inch crystal bowl and 1—Otto Tuning Fork
Total $199 (plus shipping $53.00)
Purchase Separately
1—10" inch crystal bowl $180 (plus shipping $45)
1 —Otto Tuner- $49.95 (plus shipping $7.95)
Include payment for Shipping and Handling Please

Place your order today!
Call: Ivy Hylton 301-395-0460
E-mail payment to: www.paypal.com
Click send money to: serenityliving31@aol.com
or
visit web-site: www.serenityhealingarts.com
Click Products and send payment to Pay Now Button

P.O. Box 1176-Temple Hills, MD 20757
301-395-0460

SPONSOR THE SACRED MOMENTS HEALING TOUR
SHADIAH

Rev. Ivy Hylton

"A Divine Gift of Vocal Healing Energy"

-Rev Sylvia Sumter-Unity of Washington DC

CONCERT and Workshop
A Symphonic Vocal Anointing Experience

That you do not want to miss!

Singing from her famed CD's & vibrational meditations for healing the heart, inspiring love and compassion. Join us for an intimate ethereal evening of soul stirring sounds from the spellbinding voice of **Shadiah — "A distinct voice of angelic healing qualities" Iyanla Vanzant.** Blending Nubian Age, Sacred, World & Classical elements into a body of penetrating sound waves, chants and angelic messages, destined to create Heaven on Earth. Come and be blessed by her Vocal and "Rose of Sharon" anointing experience. Come , witness and feel the pouring of high energy into the universe. Creating **Cosmotic Love Vibrations** for healing the heart, mind, and spirit, tuning into frequencies that usher inner peace into your heart and into the world.

SOUND VIBRONICS™

WITH
Rev. Ivy SHADIAH Hylton
SACRED SONIC SOUND HEALER

Sound Vibronics™
Healing Power of Sound, Vibration and the Voice
Interactive Workshop
Sound Vibration + Intent = Manifestation

Learn how to harmonize your mind, body, and spiritual life by activating the healing power of your natural voice, along with discovering how to play vibrational healing instruments for yourself and others. Rev. Ivy Shadiah, will guide you thru a series of vibrational meditations, toning and chanting exercises that will raise your body/mind/spirit vibration, balance chakra energies, release emotional blockages and raise your vibration with Brain Wave exercises. Activate The Power of Attraction to manifest, manifest, manifest!!! With sound, vibration and intention. All of life's manifestations of thought have specific and identifiable waves called vibrations. Every thought, emotional and mental state has specific vibrational frequencies that can be changed by a shift in consciousness, or thought forms. Learn to change your mental state and vibration by deliberately focusing your will on positive thoughts and intentions for positive outcomes in life.

No Singing Experience Required
"Activate the Cosmotic Love Vibration Within"

- Learn how your own created sounds can enhance health, empower your mind and calm emotions.

- Tune your nervous system, DNA and cellular structure into wellness, love, and deep levels of relaxation.

- Awaken your higher self by tuning into God's vibrational healing frequencies.

- Create a series of powerful live vibrational music meditations.

- Learn to conduct self treatments with tuning forks, singing crystal bowls, energy chimes, and angelic harps.

Purchase your vibrational healing instruments today:

Contact Rev. Ivy Shadiah @ 301-395-0460
www.serenityhealingarts.com www.thewellnesssalon.com
Email: sacredmoments7@aol.com

Follow Ivy on Twitter ~ Facebook ~ iTunes
Download or purchase Ivy's Meditation Music
www.CDBABY.COM/all/ivyhilton

Journey to the Higher Self
Spiritual Healing Retreat
with Rev. Ivy

"Rest and Relaxation are the Keys to Wellness"

A full weekend of Rest, Relaxation and Spiritual Rejuvenation at the
Heaven House ~ Berkeley Springs, West Virginia
Home of the original Hot Springs SPA
Also for your church or organization
$350.00 donation - $90 for organic food

Visit our website for schedules

www.heavenhouseretreat.com
www.serenityhealingarts.com

Healing is finding an inner communion with something greater than anything of the world. It is finding ourselves in God, finding ourselves in a spiritual peace, an inner peace, an inner glow, all which comes from the realization of God within us.

Sign up today!
all retreats are designed for plenty of time for one-on-one consultation with Rev. Ivy
call 301-395-0460
serenityliving31@aol.com

INNER WORKS
LIFE JOURNAL

HARMONY* BALANCE* HEALING

JOURNEY FOR MENTAL CLARITY, RELIEVING STRESS, FINDING SERENITY AND INNER PEACE

Journey....Mission....Awareness...
Purpose......Wisdom......Insight....
Knowledge....Understanding....
Harmony....
Balance......Healing....Guidance

The Inner Works Life Journal for Harmony, Balance and Healing is based on the concept of the Meditation Labyrinth. I have selected the image of the Labyrinth because it is the perfect concept of how to use this Journal as a part of your Journey into Inner Peace. The Labyrinth is a universal symbol that dates back over 5,000 or more years, and has also been known as the maze. It is one of the oldest spiritual life tools used for meditation, prayer, ritual, initiation and spiritual growth of humanity. The Labyrinth has only one single path to the center, and can be used for contemplation, decision making, mental and physical exercise. The concept of the Labyrinth is focused on serving as a point of concentration for balance and grounding in life. The Labyrinth is a symbol of the complexities and difficulties that life can bring on our journey through life. When you enter into the Meditation Labyrinth Journal, it represents new birth and the center represents eternal life. The intention of each page in the Inner Works Life Journal is Divine Grace in action. The effect of journaling sanctifies, beautifies, strengthens the will, enlightens the mind and inspires prayer and meditation. These are the most powerful ideals in life that one can achieve. Each word that you write in your Journal will take you closer to the center of your being, and will bring comfort to your soul. The Journal is designed to inspire and facilitate meditation, prayer, personal transformation and remembrance of what to do. The Labyrinth is a sacred spiral pattern, woven with an intention of discovering purpose and meaning in life. As you begin to write in your journal, expect to find healing, wholeness and satisfaction, as you reflect on your inner most thoughts and feelings…on your Journey into Inner Peace.

**JOURNEY...MISSION...AWARENESS...
PURPOSE...HEALING...ENLIGHTENMENT...
CLOSURE...INNER PEACE...CLEANSING...
RELEASE...REST...
I AM ONE**

_____

_____

_____

_____

_____

_____

_____

_____

_____

_____

_____

_____

_____

GIVE THANKS

**YOU WILL NEVER KNOW WHO YOU
ARE IN THE WORLD UNTIL YOU
KNOW THYSELF. John Henrick Clarke
HE WHO KNOWS OTHERS IS WISE; HE WHO
KNOWS HIMSELF IS ENLIGHTENED. Lao-Tzu**

_____

_____

_____

_____

_____

_____

_____

_____

_____

_____

_____

_____

_____

_____

GIVE THANKS

MELODIC SOUNDS BRING BEAUTIFUL AND INSPIRING GIFTS, OFFERING PEACEFUL TRANQUILITY.

_____

_____

_____

_____

_____

_____

_____

_____

_____

_____

_____

_____

_____

GIVE THANKS

HARMONY*BALANCE*HEALING
I AM SO GRATEFUL

_____

_____

_____

_____

_____

_____

_____

_____

_____

_____

_____

_____

_____

_____

MEDITATION IS THE EXPERIENCE OF THE LIMITLESS NATURE OF THE MIND WHEN IT CEASES TO BE DOMINATED BY ITS USUAL MENTAL CHATTER. David Fontana

**MEDITATION RESULTS IN EXPERIENCING
PHYSICAL, MENTAL AND SPIRITUAL
WELL-BEING. DURING MEDITATION
THE BODY IS RELAXED AND FREE
FROM STRESS AND TENSION.**

_____

_____

_____

_____

_____

_____

_____

_____

_____

_____

_____

_____

_____

_____

GIVE THANKS

AS I CONCENTRATE FULLY ON THE INNER LIGHT AND SOUND, MY SOUL RISES ABOVE THE LIMITATIONS OF MY MIND AND I ULTIMATELY EXPEREIENCE SELF-KNOWLEDGE AND GOD REALIZATION.

GIVE THANKS

LET US NOT PRAY TO BE SHELTERED FROM DANGER BUT TO BE FEARLESS IN FACING THEM. LET US NOT BEG FOR THE STILLING OF THE PAIN BUT FOR THE HEART TO CONQUER IT. Rabindranath Tagore

_____

_____

_____

_____

_____

_____

_____

_____

_____

_____

_____

_____

_____

IN MEDITATION I WITHDRAW MY ATENTION FROM THE OUTSIDE WORLD AND THE PHYSICAL BODY AND FOCUS IT AT THE SEAT OF MY SOUL.

_____

_____

_____

_____

_____

_____

_____

_____

_____

_____

_____

_____

_____

_____

GIVE THANKS

**SINGING IS A SPIRITUAL EXPRESSION
OF THE SOUL. AN OPPORTUNTIY TO
EXPRESS EMOTIONS AND FEELINGS
ABOUT LIFE AND ITS EXPERIENCES.**

GIVE THANKS

HARMONY*BALANCE*HEALING....
THE PATHWAY TO INNER PEACE,
WHICH EVERY SOUL STRIVES FOR.

_____

_____

_____

_____

_____

_____

_____

_____

_____

_____

_____

_____

_____

_____

_____

GIVE THANKS

**HARMONIOUS MUSIC VIBRATIONS CAN
STIMULATE THE BODY TO RELEASE
TENSION, STRESS, EMOTIONAL ENERGY AND
ENCOURAGE FEELINGS OF HAPPINESS
AND POSITIVE SELF-ESTEEM.**

_____

_____

_____

_____

_____

_____

_____

_____

_____

_____

_____

_____

_____

_____

_____

GIVE THANKS

**ESSENTIAL OILS AND SEA SALT BATHS
OFFER AN EXCELLENT FORM OF AT-HOME
HEALTH CARE THAT ARE BENEFICIAL
BETWEEN VISITS TO THE PRACTIONER
FOR REFLEXOLOGY, BODY MASSAGE, REIKI
AND OTHER HOLISTIC TREATMENTS.**

_____

_____

_____

_____

_____

_____

_____

_____

_____

_____

_____

_____

_____

_____

_____

GIVE THANKS

TO DO AN AROMATHERAPY BATH TREATMENT, FIRST FILL THE TUB WITH CONFORTABLY HOT WATER, ADD 8 TO 10 DROPS OF ESSENTIAL OILS INTO THE WATER. GENTLY EMERSE YOUR BODY INTO THE WATER AND THEN RELAX...

**LEARN TO ENJOY THE PEACEFUL SKY
AT NIGHT....GAZE INTO THE STARS
AND LET YOUR IMAGINATION TAKE
FLIGHT.....BREATH DEEPLY AND
ALLOW YOUR BODY TO BE AT EASE.**

_____

_____

_____

_____

_____

_____

_____

_____

_____

_____

_____

_____

_____

_____

_____

GIVE THANKS

**IF YOU ARE NOT GETTING BETTER,
YOU ARE SURELY GETTING WORSE,
BECAUSE NOTHING STANDS STILL
IN THE UNVERSE. African Proverb**

_____

_____

_____

_____

_____

_____

_____

_____

_____

_____

_____

_____

_____

GIVE THANKS

IN MEDITATION, I WITHDRAW MY ATTENTION FROM OUTSIDE OF THE WORLD AND MY PHYSICAL BODY, AND I FOCUS IT AT THE SEAT OF MY SOUL

MEDITATION IS THE EXPEREINCE OF THE HIGHER SELF AND THE MORTAL SELF COMING TOGETHER IN HARMONY AND IN LOVE = LIGHT

_____

_____

_____

_____

_____

_____

_____

_____

_____

_____

_____

_____

_____

MEDITATION RESULTS INTO EXPERIENCING PHYSICAL, MENTAL AND SPIRITUAL WELL-BEING

GOING WITHIN MEDITATION TIME
During meditation the body is relaxed
and free from stress and tension

_____

_____

_____

_____

_____

_____

_____

_____

_____

_____

_____

_____

_____

_____

_____

_____

_____

_____

As I concentrate fully on the inner light and sound, my soul rises above the limitations of my mind and I am experiencing the ultimate knowledge and presence of the realization of God

I release the fear and fulfill the desire

My thoughts are full of the vision of my hearts desires with no limitations or doubt

I release, I have clarity, and I am empowered

The healing is in the silence.......my mind is still and free from worry

_____

_____

_____

_____

_____

_____

_____

_____

_____

_____

_____

_____

_____

_____

_____

_____

Go and Rest for a while

_____

_____

_____

_____

_____

_____

_____

_____

_____

_____

_____

_____

_____

_____

_____

_____

The key to global healing starts with the
inner self. Reiki is a passage way to the
inner self for deep and lasting healing

Create a transpersonal experience and connect with your inner spirit

_____

_____

_____

_____

_____

_____

_____

_____

_____

_____

_____

_____

_____

_____

_____

_____

Meditation and prayer, provides a strengthening of intuition and deeper connections with the higher self

**Become the master teacher and spread the
light of love throughout the world.....
teach somebody how to do it**

_____

_____

_____

_____

_____

_____

_____

_____

_____

_____

_____

_____

_____

_____

Get to the core issues underneath the blocks in your life

_____

_____

_____

_____

_____

_____

_____

_____

_____

_____

_____

_____

_____

_____

_____

It is time to look deep within and take refuge for personal healing

_____

_____

_____

_____

_____

_____

_____

_____

_____

_____

_____

_____

_____

_____

_____

Take charge of your thoughts, emotions and feelings

_____

_____

_____

_____

_____

_____

_____

_____

_____

_____

_____

_____

_____

_____

Heal yourself with sound—aroma-touch-love

_____

_____

_____

_____

_____

_____

_____

_____

_____

_____

_____

_____

_____

_____

_____

_____

Restore your spirit in the hot natural mineral spring waters of the earth

_____

_____

_____

_____

_____

_____

_____

_____

_____

_____

_____

_____

_____

_____

**Learn to enjoy the peaceful sky ...
gaze into the stars...breath deeply and
allow your body to be at ease**

_____

_____

_____

_____

_____

_____

_____

_____

_____

_____

_____

_____

_____

_____

Meditate in the great, great silence as your higher self directs, guides and protects you

The Angels are calling you to listen and pay attention

Take an aromatherapy bath tonight, first fill the bath tub with twenty drops of your favorite essential oil, and then gently immerse your body into the healing waters

_____

_____

_____

_____

_____

_____

_____

_____

_____

_____

_____

_____

_____

_____

_____

_____

**Use this page to list things that
you are grateful for today**